AFRICAN AMERICAN TRAILBLAZERS

Jackie Robinson

Barrier-Breaking Baseball Legend

Avery Elizabeth Hurt

Cavendish
Square

New York

*In memory of Ray Dean, one of the finest baseball players and
kindest human beings that I have been lucky enough to know.*

Published in 2020 by Cavendish Square Publishing, LLC
243 5th Avenue, Suite 136, New York, NY 10016

Library of Congress Cataloging-in-Publication Data

Names: Hurt, Avery Elizabeth.
Title: Jackie Robinson: barrier-breaking baseball legend / Avery Elizabeth Hurt.
Description: New York : Cavendish Square Publishing, 2020. |
Series: African American trailblazers | Includes glossary and index.
Identifiers: LCCN | ISBN 9781502645517 (pbk.) | ISBN 9781502645524 (library bound) |
ISBN 9781502645531 (ebook)
Subjects: LCSH: Robinson, Jackie, 1919-1972--Juvenile literature. | Baseball players--United States--Biography--
Juvenile literature. | African American baseball players--Biography--Juvenile literature. | Discrimination in
sports--United States--History--Juvenile literature. | Baseball--United States--History--Juvenile literature.
Classification: LCC GV865.R6 H872020 | DDC 796.357092 B--dc23

Editorial Director: David McNamara
Editor: Kristen Susienka
Copy Editor: Rebecca Rohan
Associate Art Director: Alan Sliwinski
Designer: Joseph Parenteau
Production Coordinator: Karol Szymczuk
Photo Research: J8 Media

The photographs in this book are used by permission and through the courtesy of: Cover, p. 7, 53 Photo File/
MLB Photos/Getty Images; p. 4 Seth Sanchez/Icon Sportswire/Corbis/Getty Images; p. 8 North Wind
Picture Archives; p. 11 Photo12/UIG/Getty Images; p. 13 Corbis/Getty Images; p. 17 Everett Historical/
Shutterstock.com; p. 19 Addison N. Scurlock/NPG/Wikimedia Commons/File:Motto web dubois original.
jpg/Public Domain; p. 22-23 Mark Rucker/Transcendental Graphics/Getty Images; p. 26, 29 Hulton
Archive/Getty Images; p. 32, 49, 67, 69, 72-73, 84, 86, 90, 92, 96 Bettmann/Getty Images; p. 35 Walter
Oleksy/Alamy Stock Photo; p. 40 Sporting News/Getty Images; p. 43 Afro American Newspapers/Gado/
Getty Images; p. 46, 58 AP Images; p. 51 Archive Photos/Getty Images; p. 60, 76 Irving Haberman/IH
Images/Getty Images; p. 79 FPG/Archive Photos/Getty Images; p. 81 Sporting News and Rogers Photo
Archive/Getty Images; p. 98 Joe McNally /Sports Illustrated/Getty Images; p. 100 Rolls Press/Popperfoto/
Getty Images; p. 102-103 John Kershner/Shutterstock.com; p. 105 Rowland Scherman/Getty Images.

Printed in the United States of America

CONTENTS

INTRODUCTION

"42"

I t's April 15, opening day in major-league baseball (MLB). The players walk onto the field for the announcement of the starting lineup. Every player on every MLB team is wearing a jersey bearing the number 42. Since 2009, opening day in MLB has been designated Jackie Robinson Day. The man they are honoring by wearing his number (42) changed baseball; he also changed a nation.

A Player with Influence

On April 15, 1947, Jack Roosevelt Robinson—known to baseball fans everywhere simply as Jackie—began his major-league career with the Brooklyn Dodgers. He was in

The Los Angeles Dodgers line up for the national anthem on opening day 2015, all wearing the number 42 in honor of Jackie Robinson.

the starting lineup, batting second and playing first base. What made this day special, and what makes it worth celebrating many decades later, is that Jackie Robinson was the first African American in modern baseball to play on a major-league team.

Breaking baseball's color barrier was difficult. Branch Rickey, the president of the Dodgers organization, hatched a plan to make it happen. However, he faced tremendous resistance, both from the league and from a very racially segregated nation. In order to make his plan work, he had to find just the right player to be the first to stride across baseball's color line. Jackie Robinson was that man. Robinson faced incredible challenges but showed profound determination and bravery. He was not just opening up baseball to people of color. He was making a significant crack in the walls that had kept many talented people from participating fully in all aspects of American life.

Difficult Obstacles

As writer George F. Will put it, "Robinson's first major league game was the most important event in the emancipation of black Americans since the Civil War."[1] For, you see, despite the existence of the Thirteenth Amendment, which outlawed slavery in 1865, by the 1930s and 1940s, African Americans in many ways were still not free. Laws that ensured black people would live, work, and play separately from their fellow citizens not only prevented the races from mixing, but they prevented blacks from having the same economic and social opportunities as whites. Even though African Americans had been freed by the Civil War decades earlier, white Americans found many ways to keep them oppressed.

It took a long time and a bloody civil rights movement to change those laws and get legal protections for the rights of

Jackie Robinson takes batting practice in his Brooklyn Dodgers uniform at the team's spring training camp.

African Americans. Even today, the battle is still not completely won. However, there is no doubt that Jackie Robinson made a difference in the lives of all African Americans.

The words on Robinson's plaque in the Baseball Hall of Fame say that he "displayed tremendous courage and poise in 1947 when he integrated the modern major leagues in the face of intense adversity."[2] Here is the story of how he did that, why he had to do it, and the effect his actions had and are still having on baseball, sports, and the nation.

CHAPTER ONE

Slavery, Jim Crow, and a "Gentlemen's" Agreement

Baseball has long been called America's pastime. However, until the mid-twentieth century, players who played baseball professionally were not diverse. In fact, people played on different teams based on how they looked. The biggest and most talked-about division was between whites and African Americans. For decades, African Americans could not play on white professional baseball teams. Sadly, baseball was not the only thing African Americans were excluded from.

This illustration shows African American slaves harvesting sugarcane on a plantation in Louisiana.

Centuries of Bondage

In August 1619, about twenty African slaves were unloaded from a boat in Jamestown, Virginia. These were not the first slaves in the new world—slaves had been brought to the Americas since the beginning of the sixteenth century. However, these twenty or so people are thought to be the first slaves brought to the American colonies. As such, their arrival in Jamestown marks the beginning of slavery in what would become the United States of America.

America was not the first nation to import or make use of slaves, but it was one of the last to abolish the practice. Slavery was a fact of life in America for the next almost 250 years, until in 1865, the Thirteenth Amendment to the US Constitution was ratified, abolishing at last the horrific practice of enslaving human beings.

The journey to freedom, called emancipation, was not an easy one. It took years of protest and agitation by abolitionists and a bloody four-year civil war to finally rid the nation of what has been called its "original sin." The abolition of slavery did not mean all problems were solved for African Americans, though. At the end of the Civil War, America's slaves learned that they were now free people and celebrated their new freedom. However, the road ahead would be difficult for newly freed slaves and their descendants for many generations to come.

The so-called Civil War Amendments, passed in the months and years after the Civil War, gave constitutional rights and protections to former slaves and their descendants. The Thirteenth Amendment abolished slavery. The Fourteenth Amendment declared that former slaves were citizens and entitled to "equal protection of the laws" of the nation. The Fifteenth Amendment gave African American men the right

This illustration by Thomas Nast depicts the lives of African Americans before and after emancipation, and celebrates their freedom. Abraham Lincoln's image is at the bottom of the illustration, since his actions led to emancipation.

to vote (women—of any color—would not be guaranteed the right to vote until 1920, with the passage of the Nineteenth Amendment). However, though slavery remained illegal, the protections offered by the Fourteenth and Fifteenth Amendments were not enforced. After the Civil War ended, newly freed slaves discovered that while they were no longer considered another man's property, they did not have anything approaching political or social equality.

Another Kind of Slavery

Before the end of the war, Abraham Lincoln had proposed ideas on how to approach readmission of a Confederate state into the Union. Among the requirements were for people to take an oath of loyalty. Talk of allowing former slaves who had fought in the war to vote likewise flitted about; however, action was not taken until after the war's conclusion in 1865. A few short months later, Lincoln was dead and his vice president, Andrew Johnson, was leading the country. Johnson was from Tennessee, and though he was a staunch unionist, his sympathies lay with the South. He was eager to get control of the former Confederate states back into the hands of the state governments and out of government control as soon as possible. His plan for the readmission and rebuilding process in the South, called Reconstruction, required only that the new state governments abolish slavery and remain loyal to the nation. Other than that, they could run their states however they liked.

Johnson's plan gave white politicians—the old Confederate aristocracy—almost total control of creating their new governments. Black citizens were not allowed to vote for delegates to the states' constitutional conventions or in any other way participate in designing the new state governments. Soon, the leaders of the defeated Confederacy were running the new state governments. As you might expect, these new governments did not make any effort to include former slaves or protect their rights. A cartoon published in *Harper's Weekly* in 1868 made it very clear: "This is a white man's government."[1]

Several Southern states also devised laws known as "Black Codes." These codes helped in some ways and hurt in others. For instance, they gave blacks the right to marry and to own

A sharecropper and his family sit on the porch of their home in Pulaski County, Arkansas, 1935. Sharecropping was a difficult life.

property, but they denied blacks the right to serve on juries, testify in court against a white person, or serve in state militias. More disturbingly, these codes instituted a system that was frighteningly similar to slavery.

The Black Codes required black laborers to sign annual contracts with white landowners for whom they worked. If they refused or did not meet the terms of the contracts, they could be captured and hired out as forced labor. Vagrancy laws helped ensure that these contracts were signed. If a person was found not to have a job, he or she could be arrested and put to hard

SHARECROPPING

Another consequence of Reconstruction was sharecropping. After the slaves were freed, they had nowhere to live and no jobs to support themselves and their families. On the other hand, landowners who had been dependent on slaves to work their fields needed labor. So, many former slaves entered into an economic relationship called sharecropping. This allowed tenants to live on and farm a section of a landowner's property in exchange for a portion of the crop. The system was designed to make sure that black farmers never managed to get ahead. Landowners and local merchants provided seed and fertilizers and other supplies to the tenant farmers on credit. They often charged high interest rates. A poor harvest due to bad weather or insect invasions would put a sharecropper even further in debt. Laws forbade tenants to sell their crop to anyone other than their landlords. Sharecroppers were not allowed to move if they were indebted to their landlord—and most were. In short, it was yet another form of slavery. It virtually guaranteed that anyone working as a sharecropper would be trapped in a cycle of poverty for the rest of their lives. This system lasted well into the twentieth century and was the one Jackie Robinson's father, a sharecropper and the son of a slave, was working in when Robinson was born.

labor or hired out to landowners to work off their punishment. It was, quite simply, a different form of slavery. These draconian measures were justified by a deep racism displayed by many white Southerners. The editor of the *Macon Daily Telegraph* in Georgia wrote, "There is such a radical difference in the mental and moral constitution of the white and the black race, that it would be impossible to secure order in a mixed community by the same legal sanctions."[2]

In 1866, a Republican majority in Congress passed laws that protected freed slaves and limited the powers of white Southern leaders. This period was known as Radical Reconstruction. During this time, the Black Codes were declared invalid by the federal governors who had been put in charge of the former Confederate states. Slightly less harsh codes were written, and things did seem to get better for African Americans for a short time. During this period, more than six hundred African Americans were elected to state legislatures in the South, and sixteen African Americans were elected to the US Congress. Many state governments made honest efforts to protect the newly accorded rights of African Americans and to make sure they had opportunities to get an education. Sadly, however, this didn't last.

Jim Crow Moves In

In the decades that followed Reconstruction, things didn't improve much for African Americans living in the South. The spirit behind the Black Codes was reborn and continued into the twentieth century in a set of laws and social practices known as Jim Crow. The point of Jim Crow laws was to enforce, both legally and by cultural practices, a strict separation of the races in society. Black and white children attended separate schools. Black people saw different doctors from white people. Public places such as libraries, restaurants, and courthouses had separate areas for blacks and whites. Trains and buses had special areas where black people had to ride. Even restrooms and water fountains were divided by race.

There were many other laws designed to limit contact between the races. Here are a few examples of Jim Crow laws that were on the books in some states during the first half of the twentieth century:

> 1. "Marriages are void when one party is a white person and the other is possessed of one-eighth or more negro, Japanese, or Chinese blood." — Nebraska, 1911
>
> 2. "Any white woman who shall suffer or permit herself to be got with child by a negro or mulatto … Shall be sentenced to the penitentiary for not less than eighteen months." —Maryland, 1924
>
> 3. "It shall be unlawful for a negro and white person to play together or in company with each other in any game of cards or dice, dominoes or checkers." —Alabama, 1930[3]

This system of segregation was sanctioned by the US Supreme Court in 1896, in a case known as *Plessy v. Ferguson*. The court ruled that laws requiring what were known as (but rarely were) "separate but equal" facilities did not violate the equal protection clause of the Fourteenth Amendment. *Plessy v. Ferguson* was not overturned until 1954, when the Supreme Court ruled against the "separate but equal" doctrine in *Brown v. Board of Education of Topeka, Kansas*.

In *Freedom Riders*, a 2010 documentary about the civil rights period, civil rights activist Diane Nash said, "Travel in

This sign illustrates the laws and conventions that aimed to keep the races strictly separated. Jim Crow laws and practices were both unfair and humiliating to black people.

the segregated South for black people was humiliating ... The very fact that there were separate facilities was to say to black people and white people that blacks were so subhuman and so inferior that we could not even use the public facilities that white people used."[4]

Beyond humiliation, blacks faced violence if they dared challenge the system of segregation. Lynchings were tragically common, particularly in the South, from the 1880s to the 1960s. It was a practice in which white mobs would torture and murder black people, often by hanging, for the slightest offense of the social order designed to keep black people impoverished and at the mercy of whites. Lynchings

W. E. B. DU BOIS

In the decades just after the Civil War, not all African Americans were former slaves and not all were poor farmers. Those who had education and influence used it to help their fellow African Americans. The first African American to earn a PhD from Harvard University, W. E. B. Du Bois, was a professor of history, economics, and sociology. Du Bois, along with many other black intellectuals, held a meeting in Niagara Falls, Canada, in 1905. Their purpose was to find solutions to the problems of racism and inequality in the United States. While other African Americans, particularly Booker T. Washington, had advocated a slow and measured approach, the members of the Niagara Movement sought a faster way to achieve their goal. They faced resistance not only from the white community but also from some African Americans. The movement soon fell apart.

In 1909, Du Bois, along with several other Niagara members, formed a new organization. It was called the National Association for the Advancement of Colored People (NAACP). The NAACP worked and still works to advocate for the social and political rights of African Americans. Du Bois, a gifted writer, became director of publicity and research for the NAACP. As such, he was editor of the organization's magazine, the *Crisis*. He wrote many articles pointing out the evils of racism. Du Bois and the NAACP in those years made a priority of getting anti-lynching legislation through Congress.

Du Bois wrote many books, including two novels and a book of essays and poetry. He was chairman of the department of sociology at Atlanta University. He was a fellow of the American Association for the Advancement of Science and the National Institute of Arts and Letters. He was also active in the Pan Africa movement, a worldwide movement to unify and uplift people of African descent no matter where they live. He moved to Ghana in 1961 and died there in 1963, the day before the historic civil rights march on Washington.

This portrait of W. E. B. Du Bois is part of an exhibition called *Let Your Motto Be Resistance* at the US Portrait Gallery in Washington, DC.

were intended to terrorize black people and warn them of the risks of challenging white supremacy. Many people involved in these atrocities were members of the Ku Klux Klan, a group that targeted blacks and other minorities, often seen dressed in white robes and hoods that concealed their faces.

Lynchings became much less common after the Civil Rights Act was passed in 1964. However, they did not become a thing of ancient history. Michael Donald, a black teenager in Mobile, Alabama, was lynched by the Ku Klux Klan in 1981.

"We Return Fighting"

Though racism was much more blatant in the South than elsewhere in the country, it existed everywhere—even in the military.

Although African Americans have served in every war the United States has ever fought (by the end of the Civil War, around 186,000 black soldiers had served in the Union Army), for most of US history they faced discrimination and racism within the military. For most of the nation's history, military units were divided by race. African American service members were often treated like second-class members of the military as well as inferior human beings. Black service members were typically assigned combat support jobs, such as cooks and truck drivers, in the belief that they did not have the intelligence or character for combat. Even blacks who had college degrees were deemed unqualified for positions that required technical training. Once they were allowed to attain higher ranks, black officers were still not accorded the respect to which that rank entitled them. At one point in World War II, black Army officers were required to take orders from white sergeants, whom they outranked. In 1948, President Harry Truman ordered the desegregation of the military, but it would be another decade before that was fully accomplished.

Despite these hardships, African Americans served with distinction and honor in World War II, only to find that when they returned home, the nation they had fought for did not welcome them. Black service members often felt as if they were fighting two wars: one against fascism in Europe and another against racism at home.

Shortly after World War I, black intellectual W. E. B. Du Bois wrote a piece for the *Crisis*, the official magazine of the National Association for the Advancement of Colored People (NAACP). In it, he outlined the injustices soldiers returned to after fighting for freedom abroad. He closed with these words:

> *We return from fighting.*
> *We return fighting.*
> *Make way for Democracy! We saved it in France, and by*
> *the Great Jehovah, we will save it in the United States*
> *of America, or know the reason why.*[5]

By the end of World War II, however, African Americans were no closer to freedom and equality than they had been at the end of World War I. Black soldiers had fought to save the world from a tyrant rampaging in Europe yet returned home to a kind of tyranny in their own land. Racism was endemic in US society. One of the places where resistance to racism became strongest was in the sport of baseball.

A Not-So Gentlemanly Agreement

Baseball is often said to be a reflection of the nation, and America's national pastime was certainly no exception when

Josh Gibson (*standing, third from left*) and Buck Leonard (*far right, standing*) pose with the rest of the Homestead Grays, a Negro league team, at Forbes Field in Pittsburgh, Pennsylvania, in 1942.

it came to racism. Baseball was never officially segregated—that is, there were no formal rules in the management of major league baseball that said blacks could not play on the same teams as whites. However, there was something called a "gentlemen's agreement" that prevented white teams from hiring black players. The agreement was made in the period just after the Civil War.

Robinson was not the first to disrupt this arrangement. Long before there was Jackie Robinson, there was Moses Fleetwood Walker. Walker, an African American, joined the white American Baseball Association in 1884, playing catcher for the Ohio-based Toledos of the Northwestern League. However, Jim Crow laws and baseball player Cap Anson made sure that Fleet, as he was called, was relegated to a footnote in baseball history.

Anson was called baseball's first superstar. He dominated the sport in the nineteenth century. He played for and managed the Chicago White Stockings (which would later become the Chicago Cubs). When the White Stockings met the Toledos, Anson refused to play on the same field with Walker. He led other white players and managers in pushing blacks out of the game and cementing the unstated rule that major league baseball was for white men only.

That did not stop black players from playing baseball, however. Black players formed their own teams and traveled around the country playing informal games. In 1920, a group of black team owners, led by Andrew "Rube" Foster, gathered in Kansas City, Missouri, and formed the Negro National League. Other Negro leagues soon formed in other parts of the country. The Negro leagues not only provided an opportunity for African Americans to play professional baseball, but they also offered the public a chance to see high-level professional baseball players at work.

Some of the greatest baseball players were in the Negro leagues. Satchel Paige, Josh Gibson, Buck Leonard, and Cool Papa Bell are just a few of the outstanding players who spent their careers there. Other players, like Ernie Banks, Willie Mays, Hank Aaron, and, of course, Jackie Robinson, all began their careers in the Negro leagues and eventually moved to the major leagues.

The Negro leagues held all-star games and an annual world series. The success of Negro league baseball contributed to the economic success of many African American communities. Negro league games drew crowds of five thousand or more excited fans. Local businesses made money selling food and souvenirs to fans and providing food and lodging to traveling teams. And, of course, the teams provided an opportunity for fun, professional sports jobs for young African American men.

The world that Jackie Robinson was born into and grew up in was not a friendly place for African Americans. However, Robinson's tremendous athletic talent, his keen understanding of his actions, and his determination would change not only a sport but a nation.

CHAPTER TWO

A Lifetime of Standing Up to Racism

The day Jackie Robinson walked onto Ebbets Field in Brooklyn, New York, to break baseball's color barrier was not the first time he had stood up to racism. And it wouldn't be the last.

From Cairo, Georgia, to Pasadena, California

Jack Roosevelt Robinson begins his autobiography with these words, "My grandfather was born into slavery, and although my mother and father ... lived in an era when physical slavery had been abolished, they also lived in a newer, more sophisticated kind of slavery than the kind Mr. Lincoln struck down."[1] The "newer kind of slavery" that Robinson was talking about was the sharecropping

This photo of Jackie Robinson was taken around 1945, when he played infield for the Brooklyn Dodgers.

system of the post-war South. When Robinson was born in 1919, his father, Jerry, worked on a plantation near Cairo, Georgia, on the Florida border. There he made barely enough money to support his wife, Mallie, and their five children. Just six months after Robinson was born, Jerry abandoned Mallie and their children, never to return. Robinson later wrote, "He, too, may have been the victim of oppression, but he had no right to desert my mother and five children."[2]

Jerry Robinson was certainly the victim of oppression—as were his wife and children. Mallie Robinson, however, responded to that oppression in a much different way and taught her children a different way as well. When Robinson was less than two years old, Mallie packed up their meager belongings and moved the family to Pasadena, California, where her brother lived.

As a single mother, Mallie Robinson worked hard to provide for her family. She cooked and cleaned for other families. In the early years in Pasadena, things were very difficult for the Robinson family. Even though she worked long hours, Mallie didn't make enough money to care for her family. With the additional help of public assistance, and leftovers she was allowed to bring home from her job, she managed to get by. Still, there were many days when the family ate only two meals a day. Despite this, she found time for her children. Robinson recalls of her, "My mother got up before daylight to go to her job, and although she came home tired, she managed to give us the extra attention we needed."[3] Mallie Robinson made sure her children knew the importance of family, kindness toward others, and education.

Her hard work paid off, and with the assistance of a state agency, she was able to buy a modest home for her family. However, the Robinsons were not welcomed in the mostly

Mallie Robinson poses circa 1925 with her children (*left to right*), Mack, Jackie, Edgar, Willa Mae, and Frank.

white neighborhood where they lived. The neighbors tried to get them to sell their home and move away, and when that didn't work, they harassed them, calling them racial slurs and reporting them to the police for silly things. For example, a neighbor once called the police because Edgar, one of Robinson's older brothers, was making noise with his skates on the sidewalk.

It turned out that Jim Crow laws did not flourish just in the South. The practice was alive and well in California too.

The local community swimming pool was opened only one day a week for blacks to use. It was then closed the next day so that it could be cleaned before whites used it again. These kinds of insults and humiliations were common in Jackie Robinson's childhood. Mallie took the abuse with strength and grace and taught her children to do the same. Though she did not allow her children to provoke their white neighbors, she made it very clear that she was not afraid of them and would not tolerate mistreatment. This would be a lesson Robinson learned well.

For a time, Jackie Robinson became involved with a group of kids (black, Japanese, and Mexican) that formed the Pepper Street Gang. It wasn't much of a "gang" by today's standards. Other than chucking dirt clods at passing cars, they avoided violence. However, they did commit a great deal of mayhem and vandalism. They broke windows and streetlights and stole food from local markets. They ran a scam where they would hide in the local golf course and grab any stray balls they could get. Then they sold the balls back to their owners.

Robinson didn't stay a part of the Pepper Street Gang for long. He spent much of his childhood helping support his family. He had a paper route, cut grass, and ran errands for extra money.

Not Much Future in Sports

From the time he was a boy, it was evident that Robinson had a great deal of athletic talent in just about every sport he tried: baseball, football, basketball, track, soccer, and tennis. Apparently it was a family trait. His older brother Mack finished second, after Jesse Owens, in the 200-yard dash in the 1936 Olympics. Sadly, after making his country proud in the Olympics, the only job Mack could find back home in Pasadena was as a janitor for the city. When a judge ordered that blacks be allowed full access to the city's facilities, the city fired all their black employees in retaliation. Mack Robinson lost his job. His brother Jackie was more fortunate in turning his athletic skill into a source of income, but it was a long and difficult road.

Jackie excelled in baseball, football, basketball, and track in high school and at Pasadena Junior College. He was offered athletic scholarships to several universities. He was seriously considering an offer from University of California at Los Angeles (UCLA), when his older brother Frank was killed in a car accident. That sealed the decision for him. Going to UCLA would allow him to continue living at home and help his mother. At UCLA, he continued his pattern of success at multiple sports. Robinson became the first UCLA athlete to earn a letter in four sports: baseball, football, basketball, and track and field.

UCLA had, then as now, a nationally ranked and well-respected athletic program. Robinson became nationally known for his achievements there. *Sports Weekly* called him "the best ball carrier on the gridiron today."[4] He was also well praised for his work on the basketball court. When he started UCLA, he already held the national junior college record for the long jump. At UCLA, he won the National College Athletic Association (NCAA) title for the long jump. He would have almost certainly represented the United States in the 1940 Olympics if the games had not been canceled because of the war in Europe. (The United States did not declare war on Germany until 1941. However, World War II began in Europe in September 1939, and the games did not take place again until 1948.)

Jackie Robinson became nationally known when he was quarterback for the University of California at Los Angeles (UCLA) football team.

Ironically, baseball was Robinson's weakest sport in college. However, "weak" for Robinson would have been incredible for any normal athlete. He was voted Most Valuable Player in Southern California Junior College baseball and gave California a preview of his amazing base-stealing skills. According to Ned Cronin, sports editor of the *Los Angeles Daily News*, "Had it not been for the policy prohibiting Negroes in organized baseball, he would have been sought by half a dozen major league scouts."[5]

Nonetheless, Robinson knew, thanks in part to the lesson afforded by the experience of his brother Mack, that a black man had little to no future in professional sports in the United States. In his senior year, with just a few classes to go before he would have earned a degree, he dropped out of college. As he put it, "I was convinced that no amount of education would help a black man get a job." And the need for a job was pressing. "It seemed very necessary for me to relieve some of my mother's financial burdens."[6]

Though his college experience didn't do much in the way of providing for his financial future, at UCLA he did find something—or someone—who would lead to personal happiness. While working part-time in UCLA's student lounge, Robinson met Rachel Isum, his future wife. That may have been the first place Robinson had seen Rachel, but it was not the first place she had seen him. She'd watched him play ball at Pasadena Junior College and thought he was cocky and self-centered. However, it didn't take long for Rachel to get to know the real Robinson, and the two become very close. Like Mallie Robinson, Rachel believed strongly in the importance of education. However, when Robinson decided to drop out of school to help his mother, she was supportive.

After he dropped out of college, Robinson found a job as a coach for the National Youth Administration (NYA). The NYA was an agency created in 1935 by President Franklin D. Roosevelt as a part of the New Deal. The New Deal was a series of government-funded programs designed to help the country get out of the Great Depression. The NYA provided jobs for Americans ages sixteen to twenty-five. Robinson was assistant athletic director of a camp in California that helped "at risk" youth. These kids were typically from impoverished communities and might have had difficult personalities. Robinson mentored young boys and taught them sports skills.

Robinson also played semiprofessional football for the Los Angeles Bulldogs. Semiprofessional teams paid players for their time on the field but did not pay them enough to make them full-time professionals. No major professional teams at that time would hire black players. However, in the fall of 1941, Robinson was hired to play for the Honolulu Bears, a small, segregated, professional football team in Hawaii. He accepted and made the move alone. Rachel and his mother remained in California. To make extra money, Robinson got a construction job, where he worked during the week. He played football on Sundays.

Joining the Army

Football season came to a close at the end of November, and Robinson was eager to get back to California. He was on a ship home on December 7, 1941, when the Japanese bombed Pearl Harbor. The next day, the United States declared war on Japan. When the news reached him, Robinson knew that he wasn't likely to have much time at home. "Being drafted was an immediate possibility, and like all men in those days I was willing to do my part," he later wrote.[7] Sure enough, he was soon drafted into the US Army, and in May 1942, he was sent to Fort Riley, Kansas. There, he was assigned to an all-black cavalry unit.

While in the army, Robinson learned a lot and also faced more hardships. A few months after arriving, Robinson and other men in his unit took tests to go to officer candidate

Jackie Robinson was a second lieutenant in the United States Army during World War II. The military at that time was segregated.

school (OCS). This was the part of the military that trained enlisted personnel to become officers. All of the men passed. However, the army would not let them attend the program. Internationally famous African American boxer Joe Louis was also at Fort Riley in 1942, and he and Robinson became friends. Louis's celebrity status encouraged Robinson to go to him for help. Louis didn't agree with the army's treatment of his fellow soldiers, and it wasn't long before he got in touch with some powerful government officials, who put pressure on the army to allow the black men, including Robinson, into the OCS. It worked. Robinson and his fellow soldiers joined the OCS. In January 1943, Robinson became a second lieutenant in the US Army. This was progress; however, in other areas there was still work to be done. For example, Robinson was not allowed to play on the base's segregated baseball team.

That was the last time Robinson needed someone else to speak up for him. After finishing OCS, he was assigned the position of morale officer in his company. The soldiers under Robinson came to him complaining that there weren't enough seats designated for blacks in the post's exchange. The exchange was where soldiers and their families who lived on base could get a sandwich or snacks. There might be plenty of available seats in the "whites only" section, but black soldiers would still have to wait for an available seat in their section.

Robinson said he would see what he could do about the problem. He made a call to the provost marshal, the head of the camp's military police. Robinson identified himself as the morale officer of his company and explained the situation. He said that his men were in the war just like everyone else, and it seemed to him that they should have the same rights as everyone else. The major told him that nothing could be done. When Robinson continued to make his case, the major interrupted him. With his response, it became instantly clear that the major thought Robinson was white. He said, "Lieutenant, let me put it to you this way. How would you like to have your wife sitting next to a n—?"[8]

Needless to say, Robinson did not take that question calmly. He shouted so loudly into the phone that everyone in the office stopped their work in astonishment. In fact, he was so loud that the colonel could hear him all the way down the hall in his office. The major, who couldn't get a word in over Robinson's shouting, finally hung up the phone. Knowing that the colonel had heard every word Robinson said, but not what the major had said, Robinson went to the colonel and explained. Fortunately, the colonel was sympathetic. He requested that the seating situation be addressed and that the major be disciplined for his racist comments and attitude. When Robinson encountered him again, the major was much more respectful.

Things did not go so well for Robinson the next time he resisted racism in the military, however. Not long after the incident with the major, Robinson was transferred to Fort Hood, Texas. There he encountered even more racism. On July 6, 1944, Robinson was riding an unsegregated Army bus on his way to a medical appointment at a nearby hospital. He was seated next to Virginia Jones, the wife of a fellow officer. The woman was a light-skinned African American. Robinson and the woman were chatting amiably when the bus driver looked up and saw them. Thinking Jones was a white woman, the driver stopped the bus and asked Robinson to move to the back. Since the bus was unsegregated, and even still, Jones was African American, Robinson did not move. Instead, he suggested that the bus driver focus on driving. The driver drove on to Robinson's stop, but once there he got very upset and began shouting. Robinson shouted back. The driver then called the military police.

Robinson was arrested and charged with insubordination, disturbing the peace, drunkenness (even though Robinson didn't drink alcohol), conduct unbecoming an officer, insulting a civilian woman, and refusing to obey lawful orders of a superior officer. All but two of these charges—the first and the last—were dropped instantly. However, he was then tried in a military court, a process known as a court-martial. A conviction would have meant dishonorable discharge from the US Army. In addition to losing all his veteran's benefits, a soldier who is dishonorably discharged can be subject to other difficulties as well, such as problems finding jobs, housing, or getting bank loans. Nine officers, eight of them white, heard Robinson's case. The trial lasted four hours. Robinson was found not guilty of all charges against him.

Though he had been cleared of these charges, it was also apparent that Robinson wasn't going to take what he called "the Jim Crow army" without resistance.[9] The US Army was ready to be rid of this troublemaker. They sent him to Camp Breckenridge in Kentucky. There, he became an army athletics coach. Then, in November 1944, he was given an honorable discharge and sent home.

Historian and archivist John Vernon described Robinson's attitude at his trial in this way:

> His comportment revealed courage amounting almost to audacity, because even under the bleakest of circumstances, he was sustained by an unusual … determination to fight racism. In the face of determined, implacable foes such as Robinson and other black veterans, the enemy—ethnic bigotry— was going to have to give ground.[10]

Making Waves in History

This attitude did not go unnoticed. After his discharge, Robinson briefly taught physical education and coached basketball at Sam Houston College in Austin, Texas. He didn't stay there long, however. In March 1945, he accepted an offer to play for the Kansas City Monarchs, which was part of the Negro leagues. Baseball had not been Robinson's best sport in college, but during his time with the Monarchs, he proved he was quality material. In his first season of professional baseball, he maintained a batting average of well over .300. His achievements caught the attention of Branch Rickey, the general manager of the Brooklyn Dodgers, an all-white team. Rickey sent scouts to the Negro league games, telling people that he was planning to start a new Negro league team. However, his real plan was to integrate the Dodgers. He just had to find the right person for the job.

Rickey had certain standards. He was looking for someone who could obviously play the game well, but also someone educated, sober, and who had experience playing alongside and against white athletes. He entertained the thought of a few other players, in addition to Robinson. Although Robinson was talented, he was by no means the best player in the Negro leagues. In the end, it was his character and temperament that convinced Rickey to choose him.

Robinson's courage in combating racism, coupled with the dignity and self-control he had displayed at his trial, further demonstrated that he was the perfect choice. Rickey's plan to integrate major league baseball has been called "baseball's great experiment," or sometimes "baseball's noble experiment." It proved to have great and noble results, alongside extreme challenges.

Jackie Robinson is pictured here in 1944 playing shortstop for the Negro league team the Kansas City Monarchs.

Opposing Views

Those who had been opposed to integrating baseball made two basic arguments. First, they said that there were no black players good enough for the majors. Second, they said that white fans would not pay to sit in the stands beside black fans, nor would they be interested in watching black players. Robinson quickly proved both of these arguments very wrong. Fans both black and white turned out in droves to see Robinson play. Turnstiles were humming. The integration of baseball proved to be a renaissance for the sport.

That is not to say that it was easy. Robinson and Rickey had to tread very carefully, and they faced a great deal of backlash. Through their efforts, Robinson and Rickey achieved a momentous gain for civil rights and professional sports. However, it was only just the beginning. Still, by 1959, all major league teams had at least one black player. In the twenty-first century, there are many diverse professional players taking to a field or court or pitch every week on teams throughout the United States and the world.

Another Bus

Jackie Robinson's major league baseball career was profound but not very long. He played a total of nine seasons—all with the Brooklyn Dodgers. He retired after the 1956 season, while some teams still had no black players. A few years after his retirement from baseball, he announced that he suffered from diabetes. Despite his talent on the field and his undeniable contribution to the game, he was not offered a job as a manager or an executive with major league baseball.

Baseball was not the last color barrier Robinson broke. Upon retiring from the field, he became vice president of personnel for the Chock full o'Nuts coffee company. This made him the first African American vice president of a major US corporation. He also helped found, and served as chairman of the board for, the Freedom National Bank, a bank that provided loans and financial services for people of minority groups who were not able to get such services from other banks.

PARTNER AND TEAMMATE

Rachel Robinson was incredibly supportive of her husband's career and the "noble experiment" that integrated major league baseball. She took almost as much heat in the stands as he did on the field. She dealt with it with as much grace. However, it would be a great disservice to Rachel Robinson to know her only as Jackie Robinson's wife.

Like Mallie Robinson, Robinson's mother, Rachel Robinson believed deeply in the value of education. She knew that education could mean the difference between continued subjugation and liberty for minorities. She took her own education and career very seriously. She earned a master's degree in psychiatric nursing from New York University. Then she worked as a researcher at the Albert Einstein College of Medicine. After that, she went on to become the director of nursing for the Connecticut Mental Health Center and an assistant professor of nursing at Yale University.

Once when she was at work, one of her colleagues asked Rachel if she was Jackie Robinson's wife. Without even taking time to think, she replied, "No." She loved her husband and was extremely proud of him; however, she very much wanted to have a career of her own—as Rachel Robinson, not Jackie Robinson's wife. There is no doubt that she achieved that.

Along with her husband, she worked for civil rights by, among other things, hosting jazz concerts to raise money for jailed civil rights activists.

After her husband died, she founded the Jackie Robinson Development Corporation, an organization that built houses for lower-income people, and the Jackie Robinson Foundation, which provides college scholarships and leadership training for youth. She served as the chair of the foundation's board until 1996. She has received many awards and much recognition for her work on behalf of African Americans. She has also been awarded several honorary doctorates.

Rachel Robinson's hard work and success may not get as much attention as that of her husband. However, she has been just as successful, not only in building a career, but in helping give others a chance to achieve success as well.

Rachel Robinson was a loving and supportive wife to Jackie. She is also a successful and powerful woman in her own right.

Robinson was also active in the civil rights movement. The year before Robinson retired from baseball, another courageous African American, Rosa Parks, had refused to move to the back of a bus. Parks and other civil rights leaders, including Ralph Abernathy and Martin Luther King Jr., organized the Montgomery Bus Boycott, setting off the modern civil rights movement. Demands for an end to Jim Crow and protection of voting rights swept the South. Robinson stepped up to help, becoming the chairman of the NAACP's Freedom Fund Drive. Despite his increasingly poor health, he traveled around the country as a spokesman for civil rights. He met with political figures, including John F. Kennedy and Richard Nixon, and urged them to take a strong stand on civil rights. In 1967, he wrote a letter to President Lyndon Johnson in which he thanked him for his efforts to pass civil rights legislation. When two black churches in Georgia were burned in retaliation for their help registering blacks to vote, Robinson used his influence to help raise funds to rebuild them.

Many people said that because he had so much success in baseball, Robinson "had it made." He did not agree. "I won't 'have it made' until the most underprivileged Negro in Mississippi can live in equal dignity with anyone else in America," he said.[11] Though he had demolished baseball's color line and set an example for other reformers who would come after, Robinson never thought that his work was done or that our work as a nation was done.

Family Tragedy

The later years of Robinson's life were troubled. In 1946, Robinson had married his college sweetheart, Rachel Isum. Rachel completed her master's degree in nursing, and in

1965 she became an assistant professor at the Yale University School of Nursing. The couple had three children, Jackie Jr., Sharon, and David. Sadly, Jackie Jr. suffered from emotional difficulties. This was not helped by having to live in the shadow of his famous father. Of all the challenges Robinson faced, his relationship with his son was the hardest. In 1964, Jackie Jr. joined the US Army and served in combat in Vietnam. In some ways, his experience mirrored that of his father and so many other African American soldiers. "Jackie supported the war," the older Robinson wrote, "but he did not buy a system of government that preached democracy in Vietnam but had neither homes for blacks in certain neighborhoods nor jobs for black veterans in certain areas like the construction industry."[12]

Jackie Jr. was injured in Vietnam and returned from the war with a drug addiction. "When Jackie got into deep trouble, I realized that I had been so busy trying to help other youngsters that I had neglected my own."[13] The Robinsons did all they could to help their son. They entered him into a treatment program, where he was successfully treated. By the late 1960s, he was drug free, and like his father, he dedicated himself to helping others. He was working long hours on a fundraising program for the drug treatment center that had helped him. One night, in 1971, he was driving home after working late when he fell asleep at the wheel and was killed in a car accident. He was twenty-four years old.

Jackie Robinson did not long outlive his firstborn son. On October 24, 1972, he died of a heart attack and complications of diabetes. He would be remembered for breaking the color barrier in baseball, but in truth, his work for social justice for all Americans went far beyond the diamond.

CHAPTER THREE

With a Little Help from Friends

Jackie Robinson was the man who broke the color barrier in baseball. Like most heroes, he didn't do it alone, however. It took a lot of hard work by many different people to make it possible, and the effort was started many years before Robinson stepped onto Ebbets Field in 1947.

Good Enough to Die, but Not to Pitch

Despite Jim Crow laws, African American journalists were not silent about racial issues in the twentieth century. Sports were a primary platform. They formed a central part of American life. There were talented players in all leagues.

Branch Rickey was the man who signed Jackie Robinson to break the color barrier in baseball.

However, segregation made it difficult for talented players of color to achieve countrywide recognition. Before long, sports journalists took up the issue. Many black sportswriters, such as Wendell Smith and Fay Young, began as early as the 1930s writing editorials demanding an end to segregation in baseball specifically. Black voices didn't get much of a hearing in those days, though. It wasn't until white writers joined them that their cause began to truly take hold. Lester Rodney, sports editor of the *Daily Worker*, the newspaper of the American Communist Party, took on the issue as a major initiative. Not long after, white unions joined the cause.

These activists didn't stop with editorials, however. Progressive organizations and civil rights groups staged demonstrations outside major league parks. They also circulated petitions demanding the integration of America's national pastime.

By the early 1940s, these demands were growing louder. Much of the agitation came from trade unions and workers' organizations. The Trade Union Athletic Association mounted a demonstration at the 1940 World's Fair in New York City. In 1942, the Congress of Industrial Organizations (CIO) organized the Citizens Committee to End Jim Crow in Baseball. In December 1943, black actor and activist Paul Robeson spoke at the annual winter meeting of baseball owners. There, he made the case for integrating baseball. However, at the instructions of baseball's commissioner Kenesaw Mountain Landis, the owners completely ignored him. Not even one follow-up question was asked after his talk.

Nevertheless, the pressure only increased during and just after World War II. Many African Americans had fought bravely to defend their country and the rest of the world from tyranny. They did not return to a hero's welcome, however.

New York City Councilman Ben Davis was one of the first elected officials to speak up for the integration of baseball.

Black citizens had trouble finding jobs or decent housing and exercising their right to vote. They fought to defend a democracy they were prevented from participating in. They risked their lives to protect freedoms they were not allowed to share. This fundamental injustice did not go unnoticed by everyone. Much of the awareness of injustice found its expression in baseball. Rumblings for knocking down baseball's infamous color barrier grew louder.

In 1945, Isadore Muchnick, a progressive member of Boston's city council, threatened to deny the Red Sox a permit to play on Sundays if they did not allow black players to try out for the team. The team relented and allowed three black players to try out. Jackie Robinson was one of them. The Sox never truly considered hiring any black player, though. The tryouts were merely for show, and to placate progressive politicians and activists. However, the incident did bring much-needed attention to the issue.

Ben Davis, Communist Party candidate for New York City Council in the 1940s, ran with integration of baseball as one of the major planks in his platform. His campaign circulated a flyer showing a split photo: on one side was a black baseball player, on the other a dead black soldier. The text ran, "Good enough to die for this country, but not good enough for organized baseball."[1]

Not all of those who helped Robinson were politicians and social activists. Some were fellow baseball players and fans, some were friends, and some were family.

A Mother's Love

Much of the credit for Robinson's good character goes to his mother. Mallie Robinson was a single mother in a time when

Jackie Robinson poses for a family photo with his wife, Rachel Robinson (*far left, seated*), his oldest two children, Jackie Jr. (*left of Robinson*) and Sharon (*baby, seated*), his mother, Mallie (*middle, seated*), and his grandmother (*far right*).

there was little support for women trying to raise families on their own. She worked as a maid to support her four children. She herself had been born into a poor family, but she had a little education. Her parents were former slaves who owned a small piece of land in south Georgia. They urged their children to get an education. Mallie attended school up to sixth grade. In turn, she taught her father to read. Just as her parents had stressed to her the value of an education, she encouraged all her children to get an education so that they would have more options than she had.

Mallie Robinson also raised her children in a mostly white community. It was a tricky thing to do, but she managed to teach them to be proud and to stand up to racism without giving in to hate.

Like most children, there were times when Robinson grew frustrated with his mother. He thought she was too trusting, too giving even. At times, she seemed to let people take advantage of her. Sometimes, she embarrassed him with her shabby clothing. Other times, he felt guilty because she had to work so hard and at such menial jobs in order to care for him. Yet he always knew that she loved him utterly. Her love and encouragement were part of what made him the kind of person he was.

Campy's Not an Angry Guy

Branch Rickey chose Robinson in part because he thought that Robinson had the right temperament for the job ahead. It turned out he was right. However, that did not mean Robinson was an easygoing person. He was not. He was also not a man to take racism passively. After all, he had been discharged from the Army basically because he was too much of a troublemaker—shouting down a racist major and refusing to go quietly to the back of the bus, demanding his rights and proving them in court. Though in his first years in the majors some activists accused him of being too passive, he was anything but. In fact, he strongly criticized another black player for being too calm in the face of racist slurs.

Roy Campanella debuted with the Brooklyn Dodgers a year after Jackie Robinson. Campanella had been one of the Negro league players who had helped Robinson up his game

Catcher Roy Campanella made his major-league debut in 1948, not long after Jackie Robinson broke the color barrier. His career ended in 1958, when he was paralyzed in an automobile accident.

THE HEBREW HAMMER

When Jackie Robinson started playing for the Brooklyn Dodgers, Hank Greenberg was first baseman for the Pittsburgh Pirates. Nicknamed the Hebrew Hammer, Greenberg understood more than most what Robinson was going through. He was Jewish and had endured his share of prejudice in his life and baseball career. He also had to tune out racist remarks when he came to bat.

One day in 1947, Jackie Robinson and Hank Greenberg ran into each other—quite literally—on a baseball field. The Pirates were playing the Dodgers. Robinson bunted and when Greenberg fielded the ball, they collided. Fans began yelling, "Fight, fight!" but the two men did not fight. Greenberg helped Robinson get back on his feet, then spoke a few words.

After the game, reporters asked Robinson what Greenberg had said. Robinson replied only that Greenberg had given the rookie some encouragement. Greenberg retired at the end of Robinson's first season, but the two men remained friends.

in preparation for joining the Dodgers. He was the sixth black baseball player to play in the major leagues in the modern era. Robinson and Campanella were Dodgers teammates for nine years. In a situation where they were a part of a very select group—the few black baseball players in the major leagues— you might expect that they would be good friends. However, they were never close. They had very different personalities.

Despite his restraint during his first years in the majors, Robinson was impatient, intense, quick to anger, and hyper-aware of racial insults. Campanella—or Campy, as he was called—was extremely easygoing. Baseball writer Rick Swaine describes him as "gentle, unassuming, jovial, and full of life. He was a cheerleader, almost childlike in his enthusiasm."[2] This attitude often frustrated Robinson tremendously. Despite Robinson's willingness to take abuse silently for the sake of the cause of integrating baseball, he did not believe for a minute that in general a black person should stay quiet about racism. Campy's unwillingness to fight back annoyed him. "There's a little Uncle Tom in Roy," Robinson once said, referring to the derogatory name for a black man who seemed too obedient or too accommodating of whites.[3]

Yet Campy was not really an Uncle Tom. He just wasn't an angry guy. He never even got mad at Robinson when he criticized him for his passivity. In fact, Campy gave Robinson credit for the reason he didn't feel he had to be angry. "Jackie made things easy for us," he said. "[Because of him] I'm just another guy playing baseball."[4] Jackie hadn't made things all that easy, but for Campy, it was a good place to be. He never forgot that he owed that to Robinson. Though Robinson and Campy were never close, they got along well enough. Sometimes it takes more than one kind of personality to make great changes.

A Very Real Friendship

Perhaps no other person shaped Robinson's baseball career like Branch Rickey. From the beginning, Rickey saw promise in Robinson. He chose him for more reasons than just his baseball skills too.

Rickey needed a good player, of course, but also someone who could stand up to the pressure and abuse that he would certainly endure. Likewise, he needed someone who would appeal to white fans as much as to black fans. Robinson was well educated. That was important because it meant that he would be able to do a good job of representing himself and his cause to the press. He had experience playing alongside and against white athletes. This meant that he had likely already experienced racism on the field but had learned how to cope with it and succeed in spite of it. Robinson was also sober and responsible. Because he did not drink alcohol, Rickey could be sure that Robinson would not lose control and focus after a few drinks, and say or do something that would set back the effort. The fact that he was honorably discharged from the military at the rank of second lieutenant gave Robinson additional credibility with patriotic fans. By the time Rickey brought him to the major leagues, Robinson was happily married to Rachel and had a young son, Jackie Jr. This also helped assure Rickey that his star player would be as responsible in his private life as in his public life.

Robinson's passion and determination to fight racism was a part of his appeal to Rickey too. A man who was not committed to the cause of ending racism—not just integrating baseball—might not have the commitment to endure the abuse that would come his way. However, Rickey had to make sure that Robinson could keep himself under control when necessary. He had to know when to fight and when to wait until another day.

When Jackie Robinson first met Branch Rickey, he was under the impression that Rickey was interested in hiring him for a Negro league team—the Brown Dodgers—that he was planning. This had been Rickey's cover story all along. When Rickey told Robinson that he was, in fact, wanting to hire him for the Dodgers' club—starting out on their Montreal farm team—Robinson was both astonished and thrilled. Rickey asked if Robinson thought he could play for the Dodgers. Robinson answered that he could. Then, according to Robinson's recollection of the meeting, Rickey turned abruptly in his swivel chair and got right up in the younger man's face. "I know you're a good ballplayer," he barked. "What I don't know is if you have the guts."[5]

Rickey had thoroughly investigated every aspect of Jackie Robinson that he could gain access to. He knew exactly what kind of person he was dealing with. However, he still he had to make sure that Robinson could do this. Robinson recalls Rickey's words that day:

> We can't fight our way through this, Robinson … There's virtually nobody on our side. No owners, no umpires, very few newspapermen. And I'm afraid that many fans will be hostile … We can win only if we can convince the world that I'm doing this because you're a great ballplayer and a fine gentleman.[6]

Rickey explained to Robinson that this project was about much more than the box scores. It would take a tremendous amount of courage and resolve. The conversation was not an

Jackie Robinson and Branch Rickey formed a partnership that turned into a lasting friendship based on mutual affection and respect.

easy one for Robinson. Rickey threw hard questions at him, demanding that he defend his courage. Rickey, of course, was testing Robinson. He explained that racist comments would be the least of what he faced. Pitchers would throw "beanballs"—pitches aimed at his head; fans and others would try to physically attack him; his family might be threatened. Rickey wanted to know if Robinson could remain calm and control his temper in the face of all this. Could he put the ultimate goal—the successful integration of baseball—ahead of his desire to fight back?

Robinson did not feel particularly calm. He felt the heat rising in his face as he asked, "Mr. Rickey, are you looking for a Negro who is afraid to fight back?" Rickey responded in a mirror of the rage that Robinson was feeling. "Robinson," he said, "I'm looking for a player with guts enough not to fight back."[7] And that would be a lot of guts. Robinson passed that first test with honors—a preview of how he would perform in many tests to come. At the end of that first meeting, Rickey knew that he had found his man.

This was the beginning of a close friendship that would last until Rickey's death in 1965. Rickey's audacious plan would not have worked if Robinson had not been the exceptional person that he was. But neither would it have worked if he and Rickey had not been able to work closely and amiably with one another. In 1950, three years after he started in the majors, Robinson wrote a letter to Rickey, saying, "My wife joins me in saying thank you, Mr. Rickey, and that we sincerely hope that we can always be regarded as your friends and whenever we need advice we can call on you." Rickey responded by writing, "I choose to feel that my acquaintanceship with you has ripened into a very real friendship."[8]

CHAPTER FOUR

Crossing the Color Line

O n April 15, 1947, Jackie Robinson walked onto Ebbets Field in Brooklyn, New York, and changed the course of baseball forever. To get to that point, however, it had taken great effort and determination. Never could he have thought, starting on the Kansas City Monarchs Negro league team, that he would play for the Brooklyn Dodgers major league team a few years later. With his debut, Robinson made history and paved the way for others like him to reach for the seemingly unreachable.

Jackie Robinson kneels with a pair of bats
at the opening game of the 1947 season.

Struggling Across the South

After that astonishing interview with Branch Rickey in August 1945, Robinson did not go straight to the Brooklyn Dodgers. He was hired to play for the Montreal Royals, one of the minor league teams that was part of the Dodgers organization. These minor league teams were called "farm teams" because they were where the major league teams cultivated new talent. Generally, if a player did well in the minors, he would eventually join the organization's major league team.

However, before he reported to the Royals, Robinson went to Venezuela as part of a Negro league all-star team. On this trip, other great black baseball players such as Roy Campanella and Cool Papa Bell helped Robinson improve his already impressive skills. They worked on fielding, running, and hitting. Only one black player could be the first to play in the major leagues, but it was the team effort of many of the great Negro leaguers who prepared Robinson for the challenges ahead. They knew, and Robinson knew, that if this plan were to work, he would have to be not just a very good player, but an exceptional one.

Joining the League

On October 23, 1945, the Dodgers announced that they had signed Jackie Robinson to play for the Montreal Royals. Rickey and Robinson had done a great job of keeping the plan a secret. Robinson had told only Rachel and his mother. The sports press and the world of baseball were shocked to hear the news.

Major league players who opposed integration of their sport were not terribly worried, though. They did not expect much to come from the "great experiment." Bob Feller, a pitcher for the Cleveland Indians, thought that Robinson didn't have what it took for baseball because he was built more like a football player than a baseball player. Feller said, "[Robinson] couldn't hit an inside pitch to save his neck. If he were a white man, I doubt if they would even consider him as big league material." The white press was not much more optimistic about his chances. One journalist predicted that Robinson wouldn't be able to take the pressure in Montreal and would quickly give up and go back to the Negro leagues.[1] This was just the beginning of the criticism Robinson faced.

The black press, on the other hand, added pressure of another sort. One black journalist wrote, "The hopes and anxieties of the Negro race were placed squarely on the shoulders of Jack Roosevelt Robinson."[2]

Rickey played it safe. He told the press that he had no intention of being a "crusader," he merely meant to be fair. His objective, he said, was "to win baseball games."[3]

Robinson's introduction to the Royals, in October of that year, was a good preparation for his introduction to the majors—in more ways than just honing his baseball skills. Robinson never pretended it was easy. In February 1946, just before Jackie would begin spring training as a part of the Dodgers organization, he and Rachel married. He would need Rachel beside him and in the stands as he faced this crucial first test. Fortunately, both Robinson and Rachel understood just how important this test was.

Jim Crow, Again

The Royals held their spring training camp in Daytona, Florida. However, trouble started long before Robinson and Rachel arrived. The couple had to take several planes to get there. When they stopped in New Orleans, Louisiana, to catch their connecting flight to Daytona, they discovered that they had been bumped from the flight. This kind of treatment was not unusual for black people in those days, especially in the South. In addition to the inconvenience of having to wait for another flight, there was the problem of food. Blacks were not allowed to eat in the airport snack bar. They asked where they could find a restaurant and were told of a place that would make them some sandwiches. They would, however, have to take the food out of the restaurant to eat it. They decided to just wait until they reached a place where, as Robinson put it, "We could be treated as human beings."[4]

When they finally boarded, they were headed first to Pensacola, Florida, to refuel. However, when the plane stopped there, a white couple was given the Robinsons' seats. There was no hotel in Pensacola that would accept black guests, so the Robinsons decided not to wait for a flight. Instead, they bought Greyhound bus tickets to Jacksonville, Florida. The bus was empty when they boarded, and they chose seats near the center of the bus. By this time, they were exhausted, and they gratefully sank into the seats, tilting them back into the reclining position so that they could get some rest on the trip across the state. At the next stop, white passengers boarded, and the driver told the Robinsons that they had to move to the back of the bus. He called Jackie Robinson "boy." Unlike in the military, there was no law here that prevented discrimination on buses. Rage was boiling inside Robinson. He remembered the talks he and Rachel had as they were preparing for this ordeal. "We had agreed," he later wrote in his biography, "that I had no right to lose my temper and jeopardize the chances of all the blacks who would follow me if I could help break down the barriers."[5] They moved quietly to the back of the bus.

Robinson did not know it at the time, but Rachel wept softly as she sat beside him in the dark. She wasn't crying for herself, but for him. She knew just how much it cost him to swallow his pride and his rage and submit to this humiliation. Jackie Robinson had not even arrived at spring training camp, and his resolve was already being sorely tested.

When they finally arrived in Daytona, they discovered that they weren't to be treated much better there. The team was housed in a local hotel. However, the Robinsons weren't able to stay there, since blacks weren't allowed. Luckily, Joe Harris, a local black politician and activist, welcomed them into his home. At training, Robinson was not allowed to use the same showers as the other players. Again, a local black family who lived near the ballpark welcomed him to use theirs. If the white community in the South did not live up to the reputation for Southern hospitality and kindness, the black community certainly did.

New Player in Town

Robinson's fellow players weren't openly hostile to him, but most didn't go out of their way to make him feel welcome. There were exceptions, however. Lou Rochelli had expected to play second base before Robinson joined the team. Instead, Robinson was assigned that job. However, Rochelli did not resent Robinson taking what he had expected would be his place. In fact, he worked with Robinson, who had been playing shortstop, to help him tweak his moves to be more effective at second.

When the Royals played spring training games around the region, Robinson faced racism in many Southern cities. In Jacksonville, Florida, the team arrived for their scheduled game to find the stadium padlocked. There was a city ordinance against integrated sporting events. Similar things happened in Savannah, Georgia, and Richmond, Virginia. In Sanford, Florida, the game began, and the crowd seemed welcoming of Robinson. However, soon the police arrived and informed the manager that Robinson would have to be removed from the game because of local ordinances like the one in Jacksonville. The chief of police escorted Robinson off the field.

As far as the fans were concerned, many wanted to simply watch Robinson play in a game. Black fans as well as whites came out to watch him. Seeing those supportive, eager faces in the stands reinforced for Robinson the importance of what he was doing. The black fans, too, seemed to abide by an unspoken agreement. They dressed well, behaved well, and avoided responding to insults in any way that would cause trouble. They already knew the magnitude of what Robinson was doing, and they were willing to play the long game.

In the end, the white crowds came around too. Robinson played extremely well, and that was enough for them. It looked like winning was more important than color to these Southern sports fans.

Love Not Lynching

Things were much better in Montreal. The Robinsons found it easy to find an apartment; there were no bans on renting to blacks. Fans were friendly and welcoming. In this Canadian city, skin color really didn't seem to matter. It was a nice reminder of

Dodgers fans—both black and white—gather to cheer on their team against the New York Yankees in the 1947 World Series.

what Robinson was sacrificing for. Perhaps one day, the United States would be that way too.

The abuse started again whenever the team returned to the United States for games. In Baltimore, Maryland, Rachel Robinson sat stoically in the stands as people behind her shouted insults when her husband took the field. Jackie Robinson was immoveable on the diamond. Sometimes he even showed his sense of humor. In Syracuse, New York, an opposing player tossed a black cat on the field, saying, "Hey, Jackie, there's your cousin." When a few plays later Robinson doubled and scored on a base hit, he shouted to the player who had tossed the cat, "I guess my cousin's pretty happy now."[6]

Gradually, Robinson earned the respect of his fellow team members and the adoration of the fans. His talent on the field and his grace off of it did a lot to change minds. Robinson led the Royals to the league pennant that year, with a nineteen-and-half-game margin. When he scored the winning run in the Little World Series (the championship series of the minor leagues), fans were so thrilled that they chased him down as he tried to leave the stadium to catch a flight. When they caught up with him, they hugged and kissed him, and hoisted him on their shoulders for a victory lap. Sam Maltin, a sports journalist for the *Pittsburgh Courier*, wrote, "It was probably the only day in history that a black man ran from a white mob with love instead of lynching on its mind."[7]

All of this prepared Robinson for the next trial—which would be much worse—when he was sent up to the majors. There he would face the racism of an entire nation and the antagonism of the baseball establishment for which he worked.

Secret Intrigue

While Robinson had been stealing bases and fending off cats in the minor leagues, the upper echelons of baseball had been giving some thought to the issue of integrating the major leagues. Major league baseball's owners and executives held a vote on the matter at a meeting at the Blackstone Hotel in Chicago in August 1946. Fifteen of sixteen teams voted against

Safe! Jackie Robinson slides into home in a game with the Chicago Cubs.

ON THE GRIDIRON AND THE COURT

Baseball was not the only sport in which African Americans were unofficially banned for part of the twentieth century. Also, it would not be the only sport to remove those barriers in the 1940s and 1950s. In 1946—a year *before* Robinson strode across baseball's color line—the National Football League signed two black players, Kenny Washington and Woody Strode. (Both Washington and Strode had been Robinson's teammates at UCLA.) In 1950, the National Basketball Association drafted its first black players, Earl Lloyd, Nat (Sweetwater) Clifton, and Chuck Cooper. In 1950, Althea Gibson became the first African American to play in the US Tennis Championships. In 1956, she became the first person of color to win a Grand Slam tennis tournament.

So why does the integration of baseball get so much attention? For one thing, it was among the first sports to integrate. No sport had been as popular and fundamental to US life as baseball. As hard as it may be to believe now, football, although it existed, was a fairly new sport in the 1940s. The first NFL draft was held in 1936. Breaking the color barrier in baseball was a significant step. It also meant much more than just letting blacks and whites play together. It meant that the nation's image of itself included blacks and whites working together and playing together. It meant that if baseball could be integrated, so could the rest of society.

integrating the majors. The only team to vote yes? Branch Rickey's Brooklyn Dodgers. Rickey was completely on his own.

The owners and executives weren't the only people in professional baseball who didn't want to see a black player take part in the major leagues. A group of Dodgers players secretly circulated a petition agreeing to a boycott. If Robinson were on the team, they would refuse to play. They planned to present Rickey with their petition if he brought Robinson to the team. One of the conspirators began to have second thoughts, however, and leaked word of the plan.

The team's manager, Leo Durocher, was not particularly interested in integrating baseball or anything else. He was, however, very interested in making money. He pointed out to the conspirators that Robinson was an amazingly talented player who would help them win games. Winning games would mean bigger crowds and more money for the franchise.

For his part, Rickey took a more direct approach. He made it clear to the players that he had no intention of changing his plans. If they didn't want to play with a black man, they could quit.

Perhaps the main reason the boycott fizzled out was because one of the team's leaders, Pee Wee Reese, refused to sign. He was from Kentucky, and the instigators had been sure of his support. However, he was unwilling to go along. Later, he would make his statement more publicly and more profoundly.

A combination of stubbornness on Rickey's part, greed on Durocher's, and principle from Reese effectively squashed the potential revolt. On April 10, 1947, only a few days before the beginning of baseball season, the Brooklyn Dodgers announced that they had bought Robinson's contract from the Montreal Royals. It was official. For the first time in the modern era, an African American would be playing major league baseball.

Robinson was known for stealing home. In this photo, he slides home on a steal in the fourth inning of the first game of a doubleheader with the Philadelphia Phillies.

The Big Show

When Jackie Robinson walked onto the field on April 15, 1947, his wife Rachel and their five-month-old son were in the stands to support him. They were joined by a crowd of twenty-six thousand fans—fourteen thousand of whom were black. However, it wasn't a particularly good crowd for the Dodgers. It was a cool day, and there had been an outbreak of smallpox in the city. Jonathan Eig, author of *Opening Day: The Story of Jackie Robinson's First Season*, explains why fewer white fans came out that day: "White Brooklynites were not accustomed to being surrounded by black Brooklynites, and they were not eager to discover how it felt."[8] However, as the season continued and Robinson proved what a good player he was, the stands started to teem with people. The Dodgers' publicist declared that Jackie Robinson was the greatest box-office attraction since Babe Ruth.

Robinson's first major-league season didn't start off so great. He didn't get one hit in his first game. In fact, he didn't get a base hit in his first five games. He later called his first performance on the field "miserable."[9] The team's manager, Burt Shotton, kept him in the lineup, though. Robinson soon got his groove back. He finished the season with a .297 batting average and led the National League with twenty-nine stolen bases. He finished second in the league with 125 runs scored. In 151 games, he got 175 hits and twelve homers. The Dodgers made it to the World Series that year but lost four games to three to the New York Yankees. All in all, it was an awesome season for the Dodgers. Robinson was named Rookie of the Year and had earned it.

Robinson had not only disproved but *shattered* the myth that black players were not talented enough to play in the big leagues. He had also proved that people would come out to see a black player and that white fans would sit alongside black fans in the stands. However, it didn't happen overnight, and it didn't come easily.

Baseball is often called America's national pastime, but in truth, it is more than a pastime. President Herbert Hoover said, "Next to religion, baseball has furnished a greater impact on American life than any other institution."[10] If you look carefully, you can trace the history of the nation in the history of baseball. Perhaps no chapter of America's history is better mirrored in baseball than the long, difficult struggle for civil rights. When Jackie Robinson broke baseball's color barrier, he brought out both the worst and the best in his fellow Americans, and paved the way for future players in the country.

CHAPTER FIVE

⌒

The World Was Watching

Upon its introduction, Branch Rickey refused to be intimidated by those who opposed his plan to integrate baseball. Also, since he was so secretive about his plan right up until he executed it, there was little either organized baseball or the public could do to stop him once it was in action. After Jackie Robinson took the field, however, it was another matter. Haters and bigots came out to the ballpark—but so did many other people, both black and white.

"We Was Robbed!"

Before the Dodgers' first game of the 1947 season, no one knew if Jackie Robinson would actually play. The press

Fans walk into Ebbets Field
Stadium, where Jackie Robinson
broke baseball's color barrier.

thought that he might make a token appearance, though they had been cautioned to also prepare for race riots.

The crowd in attendance was amazed, however, when the lineup was announced and Robinson was listed as starting at first base, batting second. Robinson normally played second base, so his debut at first was surely surprising. However, the manager had worried that at second, he was likely to be the victim of spiking—when a runner coming into a base slides and stabs the baseman with the spikes of his shoes.

Robinson was later tested at the bat. Having hit a promising ball, he ran; however, he was called out at third. It was clear to most observers that he had arrived at the base just barely ahead of the baseman—or at the very least, he tied. In baseball, a tie goes to the runner. The umpire called him out. The call was argued by many as unjust, and any other player could have questioned it without causing problems. Things were different for Robinson, though. He gave the umpire a hard look, then turned and walked back to the dugout. A couple of white Dodgers fans shouted, "We was robbed! We was robbed!" According to Ed Silverman, who was covering the game for *Sports-Week* magazine, "The reaction of those two guys said it all. That one moment had transformed Jackie from a stranger and outsider to a Brooklyn Dodger."[1] The rest of the game was quiet.

The many African Americans who had come to the game were quiet as well. According to Silverman, black ministers in Brooklyn had warned their congregations, saying, "This is a very critical time for us, because not only is Jackie Robinson being judged, we're all being judged by how we behave at the ballpark. So we're asking you, please contain yourselves, act like ladies and gentlemen, wear proper attire, please do not drink or make any derogatory remarks. As Jackie goes,

Fans of all races and ages waited in long lines to get an autograph from Jackie Robinson.

we all go. We're all going to rise or fall together."[2] The black community took this advice to heart. They realized, just as Robinson did, that the stakes were high. This was a time to exercise patience and forbearance. If Robinson could take the heat on the field, then they could take it in the stands.

After the game, hundreds of fans—both white and black—stayed to shake Robinson's hand. All in all, it seemed like the noble experiment was going well. But the peace was not to last.

Facing Down Ridicule

Within a few months, Robinson's fellow team members had made peace with him, if they hadn't yet come to love him.

Dodgers fans were beginning to accept him as their own. However, opposing players showed him no adoration. On April 22, the Philadelphia Phillies came to Ebbets Field for a three-game series. As soon as Robinson came to bat, hate began to pour from the Phillies' dugout. Phrases like, "They're waiting for you in the jungle, black boy," and "why don't you go back to the cotton field where you belong" were among the least of the insults Robinson endured that day.[3] However, not only were the players hurling these horrible remarks at Robinson, but they insulted his family as well.

Ben Chapman, then the manager of the Phillies, egged on his team and led the chorus of abuse that spewed from the dugout. Chapman would try to defend his behavior by saying that insults and hateful heckling were just part of the game, a way to shake up opposing players. Other baseball noteworthys, such as Joe DiMaggio, an Italian, and Hank Greenberg, a Jewish player, had been ridiculed and called names when they started playing. Chapman himself had been the brunt of some very hurtful and obscene comments about his Southern heritage when he was a player. These players were, however, allowed to play. Chapman had been a very talented ballplayer before becoming a manager. However, today he is not remembered for his skill on the field. He is remembered for his venom in the dugout.

In any case, baseball was changing, as was the nation. If this kind of hatred had once been accepted, it was not going to be much longer. The "they're just joking" response to bullying and hatred was soon seen as a dishonest excuse.

We will never know what it cost Jackie Robinson to listen to this verbal assault without reacting. He later described this as being the day when he came the closest to buckling under the pressure. In his autobiography, he wrote:

Ben Chapman, here with the Cleveland Indians, was a talented ballplayer, but he is remembered more for his bullying and abusive behavior than for his sport skill.

For one wild rage-crazed minute I thought, "To hell with Mr. Rickey's 'noble experiment.' It's clear it won't succeed" ... I thought what a glorious, cleansing thing it would be to let go. To hell with the image of the patient black freak I was supposed to create. I could throw down my bat, stride over to that Phillies dugout, grab one of those [guys] and smash his teeth in with my despised black fist. Then I could walk away from it all.[4]

But then he thought about how this fight was not just for him, not just about his career in sports. It was about the fight for his people. He swallowed his anger and pride and remained in the game.

Despite the challenges and the desire to leave it all behind sometimes, Robinson stayed firm in his commitment to Rickey and the plan. His teammates, however, had made no such commitment. They knew that Robinson could not stand up for himself, so they stood up for him. By the third day of the series, the taunts had not lessened. Finally, Eddie Stanky, the Dodgers second baseman, had had enough. He erupted from the Dodgers' dugout, shouting at the Phillies, "Listen, you yellow-bellied cowards, why don't you yell at somebody who can answer back!" This moment didn't end the abuse, but it did make it very clear that Jackie Robinson had the respect and support of some of his white teammates. The press condemned Chapman and praised Robinson's restraint, calling him "the only gentleman among those involved in the incident."[5] The noble experiment was working.

A Plot Is Foiled

The Phillies were openly hostile to Robinson and showed it in the most outrageous way. However, the Saint Louis Cardinals took a sneakier approach. Some members of the team hatched a secret plot to stage a protest strike on the day they were to play the Dodgers if Robinson was in the lineup. They hoped that other teams would follow suit, and all the teams would join in solidarity in the effort to keep major league baseball white. The Cardinals owner, Sam Breadon, heard of the rumors and reported the plan to the president of the National League, Ford Frick. Frick made it absolutely clear that the league would stand behind Robinson, and any players who took part in a strike would be punished.

On May 9, sportswriter Stanley Woodward began his column in the *New York Herald Tribune* with the story: "A National League players' strike, instigated by some of the Saint Louis Cardinals, against the presence in the league of Jackie Robinson, Negro first baseman, has been averted temporarily and perhaps permanently quashed."[6] Another attempt to drive out Robinson had failed.

Foiled plots and shouting matches aside, probably the most powerful reaction of Robinson's teammates came from Dodgers shortstop Pee Wee Reese. Reese was from Kentucky, and many expected that, being a Southerner, he would be against Robinson being part of the team. Reese, however, had been supportive of Robinson from the day the man arrived at spring training. The world did not know this, however, and those seeking to stir up trouble spread rumors that Reese resented Robinson. Then one day, Reese got a very public opportunity to set the record straight. In the midst of a game, Robinson, at first base, was being badly heckled. Reese walked over and stood beside his friend, casually draping an arm over Robinson's shoulder. As Robinson later described the gesture: "Pee Wee kind of sensed the sort of helpless, dead feeling in me and came over and stood beside me for a while. He didn't say a word, but he looked over at the chaps who were yelling at me and just stared. He was standing by me, I could tell you that." In 1947, for a white Southern man to stand up for his black friend in the face of the hatred being aimed at him was a true act of heroism. This quiet show of support and defiance became an inspiration to others then and now. Reese himself never took much credit for what he did. His wife later said, "Pee Wee thought nothing of it. For him, it was a simple

Pee Wee Reese, a teammate of Robinson's and a Southerner, made it clear to the nation that he welcomed Robinson to his team.

gesture of friendship. He had no idea that it would become so significant."[7]

While Reese didn't have anything to say about his own heroism, he did say something about Robinson's:

> To be able to hit with everybody yelling at him. He had to block all that out, block out everything but this ball that is coming in at a hundred miles an hour

and he's got a split second to make up his mind if it's in or out or down or coming at his head, a split second to swing. To do what he did has got to be the most tremendous thing I've ever seen in sports.[8]

Black and White and Red in Places

All this drama was happening on the field, but not much of it made it to the white newspapers. Oddly, the nation's sports pages covered Robinson's major league debut without much fuss.

From reading the sports pages of the major papers, people might have thought that breaking the color barrier was no big deal. Most sportswriters stuck to the facts and statistics of the game and made little mention of Robinson. Red Smith, Pulitzer Prize-winning sportswriter, didn't mention Robinson until the twelfth paragraph of his piece on Robinson's first major league game. When he did, he referred to him as "that dark and anxious young man." Another Pulitzer-winning sportswriter, Arthur Daley of the *New York Times*, did discuss Robinson. However, Daley seemed somewhat anxious to reassure his readers that they had nothing to fear from Robinson. He wrote, "The muscular Negro minds his own business and shrewdly makes no effort to push himself. He speaks intelligently when spoken to and already has made a strong impression." These words, perhaps unintentionally, condescending and insulting, not just to Robinson but all African Americans. They were not surprising, though. Sadly, in those days most white people didn't expect a black person to "speak intelligently" (when spoken to or otherwise) or "make a strong impression." Neither was it surprising that the white press didn't stress the significance of erasing baseball's color line.[9]

Jackie Robinson was a hero, but it wasn't easy. There were times when he wanted to give it all up, but he stayed strong.

At this time, the media didn't spend much ink on discrimination, wherever it occurred. In fact, there was a color barrier in sports writing as well as in playing sports. Black sportswriters were not allowed to join the Baseball Writers Association of America. On the rare occasion that baseball's segregation was mentioned in the press, white sportswriters justified it with the same tired argument: there were no black players good enough to play in the majors.

Because of this lack of coverage, most Americans were mostly unaware that segregation of baseball was an issue. Everyone knew that African Americans had their own baseball league and did not play in the white majors. What most people didn't know was that there was a gentlemen's agreement among the executives of baseball to keep them out. That black people did not attend or participate in major league baseball games did not seem odd to most whites. White Americans were so accustomed to having their world to themselves that it seemed like they hardly noticed the absence of blacks. They most likely didn't know that many people had been working for years to end discrimination in baseball. Thanks to the lack of coverage of the issue, few white people seemed to care.

The black press and the Communist press, however, did make a fuss. In fact, they had been doing so for years, demanding an end to discrimination in baseball and elsewhere. When Robinson made his considerable crack in the color barrier, they covered it not only with dry facts and statistics, but with a deep historical awareness.

When Robinson was first chosen by Branch Rickey, the *Philadelphia Courier*, an African American weekly paper, wrote that Robinson "carried the hopes, aspirations and ambitions of thirteen million black Americans heaped on his broad, sturdy shoulders." The *Crisis*, the official magazine of the NAACP, called Robinson "the symbol of hope of millions of colored people in this country and elsewhere." Robinson was not merely a symbol of hope to black Americans, according to the *Crisis* editorialists. They generously wrote that "the hopes of millions of fair-minded white Americans who want to see every American get a chance regardless of race, creed, or color" were also resting on Robinson's mighty shoulders.[10]

At Home and in the Stands

Fans in the stands and those following the games at home on the radio responded to Robinson in much the same way his fellow players did. At first, many white fans joined in the heckling and harassment that Robinson had to endure. As the season progressed and Robinson's playing improved, however, baseball fans began to see that he really was a great ballplayer. They soon saw the old argument that blacks weren't good enough for the majors for the rubbish that it was. Jackie Robinson had broken the color barrier in baseball, won over his fellow players, Dodgers fans, and to some degree the rest of the nation. From the stands and in the press, Robinson looked heroic and victorious. However, the reality in life was a little different.

Though Robinson was accepted on the field, and black Americans had seen one powerful racial barrier broken down, most of the nation was still segregated. Black Americans who were not Jackie Robinson were still second-class citizens. Even Robinson himself found that while he might have been accepted as a ballplayer, he and his family were not welcomed as neighbors. When he and Rachel tried to buy a home in nice neighborhoods in Connecticut and New York,

ROBINSON VS. ROBESON

Integrating baseball was not the only drama going on in the United States in the years immediately following World War II. In 1948, members of the US House of Representatives formed the House Un-American Activities Committee (HUAC). The focus of HUAC was to expose US citizens who had what the committee considered subversive views or behaviors, even when those activities were legal. Many people were also accused of being communist sympathizers. Communism was seen as the opposite of the United States' democracy. Many people in US government did not like it. The HUAC often tried to create divisions among citizens by forcing them to testify against one another in hearings. (Ironically, this was also a technique commonly used by the Soviet Union, the biggest communist government at that time.)

Paul Robeson was an African American singer, actor, and civil rights activist. He was one of the earliest and most vocal supporters of integrating baseball. Robeson had spent time in Russia and had been impressed with the fact that his skin color did not seem to matter there. When Robeson was asked about the possibility of war between the United States and the Soviet Union, he suggested that African Americans would be unwilling to fight for the United States in the event of such a war. He said, "It is unthinkable that American Negroes could go to war on behalf of those who oppressed us for generations."[11] The HUAC investigated him. The committee invited Jackie Robinson to testify against him.

Robinson and Robeson had very different political views. Robeson was indeed a communist sympathizer. Robinson was a liberal Republican. The HUAC hoped to get Robinson to publicly denounce Robeson. This would, they thought, drive a wedge between African Americans. However, while the two men disagreed on several things, they did not disagree on two important issues: the fundamental right of Americans to freedom of speech, and the imperative of civil rights. Rather than condemn the singer, Robinson said, "Robeson has a right to his personal views, and if he wants to sound silly when he expresses them in public, that is his business and not mine."[12]

Adoring fans even climbed over the back of the dugout to get Jackie Robinson's autograph.

they found that the asking price for the home they wanted suddenly increased. This was a common technique used to prevent African Americans from buying property in white neighborhoods. This way, the whites could say that the reason no blacks lived in their neighborhood wasn't racism. Blacks simply couldn't afford the houses. When the Robinsons offered to pay the new, higher price, they were told that the property was no longer for sale. Breaking the color barrier in baseball was a huge step for African Americans, but it was just a start.

CHAPTER SIX

Still Bashing Barriers

There have been many milestones in America's struggle to provide equal rights for all citizens. In the twenty-first century, there will no doubt be more. However, Jackie Robinson's courage and determination opened doors for others to tackle the seemingly impossible with a similar mindset. He might not have been the first to challenge segregation in sports, but he crossed a line that echoed throughout America and continues to resound today.

Silent No More

As hard as it was at times, Jackie Robinson never strayed from the agreement he made with Branch Rickey. He faced

Jackie Robinson poses with his plaque at his induction into the Baseball Hall of Fame in 1962.

tremendous abuse with silence, even though there were plenty of times he wanted to fight back. The plan paid off. By the end of his first season, Robinson was named baseball's Rookie of the Year. He was also ranked as the nation's second most–admired man in a national poll. (The first was singer Bing Crosby.) In 1949, he earned the National Baseball League's most valuable player award. That same year, his agreement with Rickey came to an end. Robinson spent much of the rest of the time on the team being himself and expressing his opinions however he liked. Many years later, Rickey told Robinson how he came to this decision:

> I knew ... That while the wisest policy for Robinson during those first two years was to turn the other cheek and not fight back, there were many in baseball who would not understand his lack of action. They could be made to respect only the fighting back, the things that are signs of courage to men who know courage only in its physical sense.[1]

Robinson had received and would continue to receive criticism for his silence during those first two years. By agreeing to be silent and passive in the face of horrific abuse, to some, Robinson presented an image of the passive, nonthreatening black man—sometimes called an "Uncle Tom." This was an image that white America could accept. For many blacks, it seemed that Branch Rickey had not so much opened baseball (and by extension American society) to African Americans, but made it clear that American society was open only to a particular kind of black person. To truly break down racial barriers, African Americans would have to be accepted on their own terms.

Once Branch Rickey's gag order was removed, the country got a chance to see who Robinson really was. It was clear he was not, as sportswriter Arthur Daley put it, someone who "minds his own business and makes no effort to push himself."[2] In fact, he was quite the opposite. People got to know the man who, as a soldier, was willing to face a court-martial rather than quietly submit to racism, and the man who shouted down a racist superior officer in defense of his soldiers. Unlike the quiet, calm person he seemed to be in those first two years, the real Jackie Robinson was aggressive, combative, and often angry. He was quick to respond to slights and offenses, and he was more than willing to speak up about injustice. He was called a troublemaker and a rabble-rouser. Many people said he had changed. He had not. He was simply free to be himself. He would have plenty of opportunities in the coming years to do so. As the civil rights movement gathered steam, Robinson joined in. His courageous stand on and off the baseball diamond inspired others to speak out against injustice and demand their rights.

Robinson's career ended in 1956. He left the major leagues with a tremendous list of accomplishments. He had won six pennants with the Dodgers. He had also been named the league's most valuable player twice. However, his legacy expanded across the baseball diamond and beyond generations.

Get Used to Me

It took twelve years for all of baseball's major league teams to integrate. The Boston Red Sox were the last, adding Elijah "Pumpsie" Green to the roster in 1959. By that time, most sports were integrated. However, much of society was not. Other sports were likewise facing struggles.

In 1966, the boxer Muhammad Ali was drafted to serve in the Vietnam War. He refused on the grounds of his religious convictions as a black Muslim. He said:

Boxing champion Muhammad Ali trains for a bout with Jimmy Ellis, a few days after the US Supreme Court threw out his conviction for draft evasion.

My conscience won't let me go shoot my brother, or some darker people, or some poor hungry people in the mud for big powerful America ... Little babies and women and children. How can I shoot them poor people? Just take me to jail.[3]

Ali was banned from boxing, stripped of his boxing title, and denied a visa that would have allowed him to box in other countries. He was arrested and convicted of draft avoidance. In 1971, the US Supreme Court eventually agreed with Ali's claim that his religion meant that he was a conscientious objector, and they overturned his conviction.

Jackie Robinson did not agree with Ali's position on the Vietnam War. However, he never denied an American of any color a right to have their say. Ali once said, "I am America. I am the part you won't recognize. But get used to me—black, confident, cocky; my name, not yours; my religion, not yours; my goals, my own. Get used to me." Jackie Robinson might have said the same thing.[4]

Raising a Fist

Despite all the progress that has been made, African Americans are still struggling to be heard. At the 1968 Olympics in Mexico City, US athletes Tommie Smith and John Carlos, both African Americans, earned medals in the 200-meter sprint. At the time, the United States was painfully divided over issues such as civil rights and the Vietnam War. Carlos and Smith approached the podium to accept their medals wearing no shoes, but only socks to protest poverty. They wore beads and scarves to protest lynching. Carlos unzipped his jacket (in a breach of Olympic etiquette) to show support

US athlete Kristi Castlin (*center*) wins the women's 100-meter hurdles in the semifinal heats at the 2016 Rio Olympics. Today, thanks to pioneers like Jackie Robinson, African American athletes have become commonplace.

for working-class people, black *and* white. When the national anthem began, both men bowed their heads and raised their fists in the Black Power salute. They explained later that they were making a statement for human rights. It was a powerful and emotional moment.

Smith and Carlos were suspended from the US Olympic team. When they returned home, they received anonymous death threats and were vilified in the press. They had some support, though. The US women who ran in the 400-meter relay dedicated their victory to Carlos and Smith.

FOLLOWING IN
JACKIE'S FOOTSTEPS

Although Jackie Robinson was the first African American to take the major league baseball field in April 1947, three months later, in July, the Cleveland Indians signed Larry Doby, who had been playing for the Newark Eagles of the Negro leagues. Other African American baseball players soon followed Robinson and Doby to the majors. In August, Don Bankhead became the first black pitcher in the majors. At the opening of the 1948 season, Roy Campanella joined the Dodgers to become the first African American to catch in the majors. In July of that year, Negro league superstar Satchel Paige made the move up.

Over the next few decades, the roster of superstar baseball players included as many nonwhite players as white ones—Willie Mays, Hank Aaron, Roberto Clemente (who was Puerto Rican), Darryl Strawberry, Barry Bonds, Ken Griffey Jr., Tony Gwynn, Derek Jeter, Frank Thomas ... the list goes on.

Meanwhile, in the latter twentieth and twenty-first centuries, many nonwhite athletes have made their mark in other sports—Althea Gibson, Arthur Ashe, and Serena Williams in tennis; Lee Elder and Tiger Woods in golf; Muhammad Ali, George Foreman, Sugar Ray Leonard, and Mike Tyson in boxing; LeBron James, Kobe Bryant, Michael Jordan, and Magic Johnson in basketball; Jim Brown, Walter Payton, Herschel Walker, Lynn Swann, Tony Dorsett, Anthony "Refrigerator" Perry, and Cam Newton in football. Today, roughly 70 percent of National Football League (NFL) players are black.

USA gold medalist Tommie Smith (*center*) and bronze medalist John Carlos (*right*) protest injustice with Black Power salutes at the 1968 Olympic Games in Mexico City, Mexico.

Today, neither man has any regrets about their protest. In a 2008 interview with *Smithsonian* magazine, Carlos said, "I went up there as a dignified black man and said: 'What's going on is wrong,'" and Smith called their protest, "a cry for freedom and for human rights. We had to be seen because we couldn't be heard."[5]

An Eloquent Silence

Jackie Robinson stood up to segregation in baseball with silence. Today, another athlete is challenging racism in the same way. In 2016, Colin Kaepernick was one of best players in the NFL. During the 2016 season, when the national anthem was played before the game, he did not stand and salute the flag. Instead, he knelt on one knee. This gesture was intended to protest racial injustice. It was not meant as disrespect to his country. It was meant to call attention to what needed to be fixed. Many of his teammates and players on other teams joined him in this action.

Kaepernick's silent protest was misunderstood and misrepresented. In a nation where the right to dissent is written into the US Constitution, his actions were not seen as constitutionally protected free speech. Instead, many saw Kaepernick's gesture as unpatriotic. Many people, including top government officials, spoke out harshly against him, calling for him and any other players who refused to stand for the anthem to be fired. Many others have supported him, including military veterans and police officers.

Jackie Robinson is no longer around to comment on Kaepernick, but he likely would have supported him. Close to the end of his life, Robinson described his feelings as he stood on the field at the beginning of the 1947 World Series. The

A crowd of happy fans, coming from diverse backgrounds, gathers to cheer on their team—the Chicago Cubs—in what is still the nation's pastime.

flag fluttered in the breeze, and the band struck up the national anthem: "As I write this twenty years later, I cannot stand and sing the anthem. I cannot salute the flag; I know that I am a black man in a white world. In 1972, in 1947, at my birth in 1919, I know I never had it made."[6]

No doubt many African Americans agree, as further struggle continues in the twenty-first century. Yet they can look back at Jackie Robinson and see the barrier he broke. They can draw inspiration from the many other black athletes who are not only able to play sports, but able to speak up about injustice, at least in part, because of him.

What America Can Be

In 2016 Barack Obama, the nation's first African American president, hosted the Chicago Cubs at the White House to celebrate their 2015 National League Championship. It was in the last few days of his historic presidency. He said:

> Sometimes it's not enough just to change laws. You've got to change hearts. And sports has a way sometimes of changing hearts in a way that politics or business doesn't … when you see this group of folks of different shades and different backgrounds, and coming from different communities and neighborhoods all across the country, and then playing as one team and playing the right way, and celebrating each other and being joyous in that, that tells us a little something about what America is and what America can be.[7]

Jackie Robinson stood up for racial equality when he was alive. He still inspires others to do the same today.

By smashing baseball's color barrier, Jackie Robinson changed the hearts and minds of many in a nation. There is still a long way to go to achieve social justice and equality for all Americans, but when many people of different backgrounds come together in America today for a common cause or to share the joy of a diverse sports game, we have Jackie Robinson to thank.

CHRONOLOGY

1919 Jack Roosevelt Robinson is born in Cairo, Georgia.

1920 Robinson's mother moves the family to Pasadena, California.

1937 Robinson enrolls in Pasadena Junior College.

1939 Robinson enrolls in UCLA.

1940 Robinson meets his future wife, Rachel Isum.

1942 Robinson is drafted into the United States Army.

1944 Robinson is acquitted in a court-martial in the US Army.

1944 Robinson is given an honorable discharge from the US Army.

1944 Robinson joins the Kansas City Monarchs.

1945 Robinson signs with the Montreal Royals, a Brooklyn Dodgers farm team.

1946 Robinson and Rachel Isum marry in Los Angeles.

1947 Robinson plays with the Brooklyn Dodgers, becoming the first black major league player in modern history.

1957 Robinson retires from baseball and become the Vice President of Personnel Relations for Chock full o'Nuts.

1962 Robinson is inducted into the Baseball Hall of Fame.

1965 Robinson cofounds Freedom National Bank, the largest black-owned and -operated bank in the state of New York.

1972 Robinson dies in Stamford, Connecticut.

GLOSSARY

abolition The end of an official practice, institution, or law, as in slavery.

agitation Arousing the attention and concern of the public and demanding action in response to an injustice.

archivist A scholar who is in charge of collecting, organizing, and storing historic documents and records.

aristocracy A class of a society considered to be superior to other members; a government run by this class.

Black Power A movement during the 1960s and 1970s that promoted equality for African Americans, usually through a more militant approach.

box score A final score and tally of a baseball game, listing the statistics for each player.

condescending Exhibiting a patronizing or superior attitude.

Congress of Industrial Organizations (CIO) An alliance of labor unions in the US and Canada, formed in 1935. In 1955, it merged with the American Federation of Labor (AFL) to form the AFL-CIO.

echelon Rank or level in an organization, company, or society.

emancipation Liberation, particularly the freeing of a person from slavery.

forbearance Self-control.

gag order A ruling issued by a judge that prevents the people involved in a case from discussing it. Informally used to indicate any demand for silence about a particular issue.

Grand Slam In tennis, the four most important tournaments of the year, including the Australian Open, the French Open, Wimbledon, and the US Open.

gridiron A slang term for a football field.

integrate To mix racial groups in a reversal of segregation.

Ku Klux Klan A terrorist organization and hate group that advocates for white supremacy (also known as the KKK).

letter An award, usually consisting of a monogram of the school's initials, awarded to an individual who excels in a particular field, usually a sport.

lynch To murder by mob, without a proper trial, usually by hanging.

manager In baseball, the equivalent of a head coach in other sports, who manages the games and makes decisions about game strategy, training, and lineup (also called field manager).

momentous Extremely important or significant, particularly in causing change or determining the course of the future.

PhD Doctor of Philosophy, an advanced degree awarded in for study and research in an academic field.

platform A set of policies endorsed by a political candidate, campaign, or party.

progressive Relating to a political position or movement that favors social reform by means of governmental policy.

Pulitzer Prize A prestigious yearly award granted to honor excellence in American journalism and other literature.

renaissance A period of renewed interest in something, a rebirth.

segregation A system of enforced separation of racial groups.

solidarity Mutual agreement or support among members of a group, usually in aid of a cause or in response to injustice.

subjugation The act of keeping a person or people under control.

turnstile A revolving gate that allows one person at a time to enter a place or event where admission is charged or attendees are counted, such as a sporting event, concert, or mass transit system.

visa An indication on a passport that allows the person to leave or enter a country legally.

SOURCES

INTRODUCTION

1. George F. Will, *Bunts* ((New York: Touchstone, 1998), 87.

2. National Baseball Hall of Fame, "Remembering Jackie," accessed August 2017, https://baseballhall.org/discover-more/stories/baseball-history/remembering-jackie.

CHAPTER ONE

1. Library of Congress, Thomas Nast, "This is a White Man's Government," wood engraving https://www.loc.gov/item/98513794.

2. Dan T. Carter, *When the War Was Over: The Failure of Self-Reconstruction in the South, 1865–1867* (Baton Rouge, LA: Louisiana State University Press, 1985), 216.

3. Smithsonian National Museum of American History, "Separate Is Not Equal: Brown v. Board of Education," http://americanhistory.si.edu/brown/history/1-segregated/detail/jim-crow-laws.html.

4. Diane Nash, PBS *American Experience*, "Freedom Riders: Jim Crow Laws," https://www.pbs.org/wgbh/americanexperience/features/freedom-riders-jim-crow-laws.

5. W. E. B. Du Bois, "Returning Soldiers," The *Crisis*, May 1919, page 14.

CHAPTER TWO

1. Jackie Robinson, *I Never Had It Made: An Autobiography*, as told to Alfred Duckett (Copyright by Rachel Robinson. New York: HarperCollins, 1995), 3.

2. Ibid., 4.

3. Ibid., 5.

4. Jules Tygiel, *Baseball's Great Experiment: Jackie Robinson and His Legacy* (New York: Oxford University Press, 1997), 60.

5. Ibid.

6. Robinson, *Never*, 11.

7. Ibid., 12.

8. Ibid., 14.

9. Ibid., 13.

10. John Vernon, "Jim Crow, Meet Lieutenant Robinson," *Prologue*, Spring 2008, https://www.archives.gov/publications/prologue/2008/spring/robinson.html.

11. Michael G. Long, *Beyond Home Plate: Jackie Robinson on Life after Baseball*, (Syracuse, NY: Syracuse University Press, 2013), 75.

12. Robinson, *Never*, 157.

13. Ibid., 154.

CHAPTER THREE

1. David Falkner, *Great Time Coming: The Life of Jackie Robinson from Baseball to Birmingham* (New York: Touchstone: 1995), 113.

2. Rick Swaine, "Roy Campanella," Society for American Baseball Research, https://sabr.org/bioproj/person/a52ccbb5.

3. Roger Kahn, *The Boys of Summer* (New York, NY: Perennial Classics, 1998), 327.

4. Rick Swaine, "Roy Campanella."

5. Robinson, *Never*, 31.

6. Ibid, 32.

7. Ibid, 33.

8. Jackie Robinson and Branch Rickey, correspondence, Smithsonian.com, https://www.smithsonianmag.com/history/document-deep-dive-the-heartfelt-friendship-between-jackie-robinson-and-branch-rickey-19817525.

CHAPTER FOUR

1. Robinson, *Never*, 36.

2. Falkner, 118.

3. Arnold Rampersad, *Jackie Robinson: A Biography* (New York: Ballantine, 1997), 131.

4. Robinson, *Never*, 39.

5. Ibid., 41.

6. Peter Golenbock, *Bums: An Oral History of the Brooklyn Dodgers* (Mineola, NY: Dover, 2010), 130.

7. Jewish Montreal of Yesterday, Jewish Public Library Archives, "Number 42," April 10, 2013, http://www.jewishpubliclibrary.org/blog/?p=1892.

8. Jonathan Eig, *Opening Day: The Story of Jackie Robinson's First Season* (New York: Simon & Schuster, 2007), 52.

9. Robinson, *Never*, 57.

10. Library of Congress, "At the Ballpark," accessed August 15, 2018, https://www.loc.gov/exhibitions/baseball-americana/about-this-exhibition/at-the-ballpark.

CHAPTER FIVE

1. John Florio and Ouisie Shapiro, "Revisiting Jackie Robinson's Major-League Début 70 Years Later," *New Yorker*, April 15, 2017, https://www.newyorker.com/news/sporting-scene/revisiting-jackie-robinsons-major-league-debut-seventy-years-later.

2. Ibid.

3. Robinson, *Never*, 59.

4. Ibid., 60.

5. David Krell, *"Our Bums": The Brooklyn Dodgers in History, Memory and Pop Culture* (Jefferson, North Carolina: McFarland, 2015), 92.

6. Warren Corbett, "The 'Strike' Against Jackie Robinson: Truth or Myth?" Society for Baseball Research, accessed August 10, 2018, https://sabr.org/research/strike-against-jackie-robinson-truth-or-myth.

7. Ira Berkow, "Two Men Who Did the Right Thing," *New York Times*, November 2, 2005, https://www.nytimes.com/2005/11/02/sports/baseball/two-men-who-did-the-right-thing.html.

8. Roger Kahn, *The Boys of Summer* (New York: Perennial Classics, 1998), 325–326.

9. Christopher Lamb, "Jackie Robinson and the Press," Huffington Post, April 10, 2013. https://www.huffingtonpost.com/christopher-lamb/jackie-robinson_b_3038540.html.

10. Bill L. Weaver, "The Black Press and the Assault on Professional Baseball's 'Color Line,' October, 1945–April, 1947," *Phylon* 40, no. 4 (1979), 303–17. doi:10.2307/274527.

11. Peter Feuerherd, "Jackie Robinson vs Paul Robeson: A Double Play for the Ages," *JSTOR Daily*, January 31, 2017, https://daily.jstor.org/jackie-robinson-v-paul-robeson-a-double-play-for-the-ages.

12. Robinson, *Never*, 83.

CHAPTER SIX

1. Robinson, *Never*, 78-79.

2. Christopher Lamb, "Jackie Robinson and the Press."

3. Krishnadev Calamur, "Muhammad Ali and Vietnam," *The Atlantic*, June 4, 2016. https://www.theatlantic.com/news/archive/2016/06/muhammad-ali-vietnam/485717.

4. Ibid.

5. David Davis, "Olympic Athletes Who Took a Stand," *Smithsonian*, August 2008. https://www.smithsonianmag.com/articles/olympic-athletes-who-took-a-stand-593920.

6. Robinson, *Never*, xxiv.

7. Paul Sullivan, "President Obama's Words of Unity Inspire Cubs during White House Celebration," *Chicago Tribune*, January 18, 2017. http://www.chicagotribune.com/sports/baseball/cubs/ct-obama-sports-cubs-white-house-spt-0117-20170116-story.html.

FURTHER INFORMATION

BOOKS

Bailey, Budd. *Jackie Robinson: Breaking Baseball's Color Barrier*. Game-Changing Athletes. New York: Cavendish Square, 2016.

Cox, Joe. *A Fine Team Man: Jackie Robinson and the Lives He Touched*. Guilford, CT: Lyons Press, 2019.

Lord, Bette Bao. *In the Year of the Boar and Jackie Robinson*. New York: HarperCollins, 2019. Reprint.

Rappaport, Doreen. *42 Is Not Just a Number*. Somerville, MA: Candlewick, 2017.

Robinson, Jackie. *I Never Had It Made: An Autobiography*. New York: HarperCollins, 1995.

WEBSITES

The Jackie Robinson Foundation
http://jackierobinson.org

In addition to information about the philanthropic work done by the organization, the official website of the Jackie Robinson Foundation is a great source of information about Robinson's life and work, on and off the diamond.

National Baseball Hall of Fame
http://baseball.org

The website of the National Baseball Hall of Fame is filled with enough history and archival material (including photos) to keep baseball fans happy during the entire offseason.

Society for American Baseball Research
http://sabr.org

The website of the Society for American Baseball Research (which is open to all visitors, not just researchers) has articles, statistics, and a digital library for baseball fans who can't get enough of the facts and figures of the nation's pastime.

MUSEUMS

Jackie Robinson Museum
One Hudson Square
75 Varick Street (@ Canal Street)
New York, NY 10013

National Baseball Hall of Fame and Museum
25 Main Street
Cooperstown, NY 13326

**National Museum of African American
History and Culture**
1400 Constitution Ave.
Washington, DC 20560

Negro Leagues Baseball Museum
1616 East 18th Street
Kansas City, MO 64108

BIBLIOGRAPHY

Barra, Allen. "What Really Happened to Ben Chapman, the Racist Baseball Player in *42*?" *Atlantic*, April 15, 2013. https://www.theatlantic.com/entertainment/archive/2013/04/what-really-happened-to-ben-chapman-the-racist-baseball-player-in-i-42-i/274995.

Berkow, Ira. "Two Men Who Did the Right Thing." *New York Times*, November 2, 2005. https://www.nytimes.com/2005/11/02/sports/baseball/two-men-who-did-the-right-thing.html.

Blackistone, Kevin B. "It's Time for Baseball to Acknowledge Cap Anson's Role in Erecting Its Color Barrier." *Washington Post*, December 2, 2015. https://www.washingtonpost.com/sports/nationals/its-time-for-baseball-to-acknowledge-cap-ansons-role-in-erecting-a-color-barrier/2015/12/02/b9b97eb8-9916-11e5-94f0-9eeaff906ef3_story.html?utm_term=.892ab5f2081e

Bouie, Jamelle. "Violence and Economic Mobility in the Jim Crow South." *Nation*, July 29, 2011. https://www.thenation.com/article/violence-and-economic-mobility-jim-crow-south.

Brown, DeNeen L. "They Didn't #TaketheKnee: The Black Power Protest that Shook the World in 1968." *Washington Post*, September 24, 2017. https://www.washingtonpost.com/news/retropolis/wp/2017/09/24/they-didnt-

takeaknee-the-black-power-protest-salute-that-shook-
the-world-in-1968/?utm_term=.314d5264a31d.

Calamur, Krishnadev. "Muhammad Ali and Vietnam."
Atlantic, June 4, 2016. https://www.theatlantic.com/news/
archive/2016/06/muhammad-ali-vietnam/485717.

Davis, David. "Olympic Athletes Who Took a Stand."
Smithsonian, August 2008. https://www.smithsonianmag.
com/articles/olympic-athletes-who-took-a-stand-593920.

Du Bois, W. E. B. "Returning Soldiers." *Crisis*, May 1919.
https://library.brown.edu/cds/repository2/repoman.
php?verb=render&id=1295986616593750&view=
pageturner&pageno=14.

Falkner, David. *Great Time Coming: The Life of Jackie Robinson
from Baseball to Birmingham*. New York: Touchstone, 1995.

Feuerherd, Peter. "Jackie Robinson vs Paul Robeson: A
Double Play for the Ages." *JSTOR Daily*, January 31,
2017. https://daily.jstor.org/jackie-robinson-v-paul-
robeson-a-double-play-for-the-ages.

Florio, John, and Ouisie Shapiro. "Revisiting Jackie
Robinson's Major-League Début 70 Years Later." *New
Yorker*, April 15, 2017. https://www.newyorker.com/news/
sporting-scene/revisiting-jackie-robinsons-major-league-
debut-seventy-years-later.

Hanc, John. "Document Deep Dive: The Heartfelt
Friendship between Jackie Robinson and Branch
Rickey." *Smithsonian*, April 10, 2013. https://www.

smithsonianmag.com/history/document-deep-dive-
the-heartfelt-friendship-between-jackie-robinson-and-
branch-rickey-19817525.

Jaffe, Jay. "And Then the Barrier Broke: Remembering
Jackie Robinson's First 10 Days as a Big Leaguer."
Sports Illustrated, April 14, 2017. https://www.si.com/
mlb/2017/04/14/jackie-robinson-day-first-ten-days.

Jewish Montreal of Yesterday: Jewish Public Library
Archives. "Number 42," April 10, 2013. http://www.
jewishpubliclibrary.org/blog/?p=1892.

Kahn, Roger. *The Boys of Summer*. New York: Perennial, 1998.

———. *Rickey and Robinson: The True, Untold Story of the
Integration of Baseball*. Emmaus, PA: Rodale, 2014.

Lamb, Christopher. "Jackie Robinson and the Press."
Huffington Post, April 10, 2013. https://www.
huffingtonpost.com/christopher-lamb/jackie-
robinson_b_3038540.html.

McCue, Andy. "Branch Rickey." The American Society
of Baseball Research. https://sabr.org/bioproj/
person/6d0ab8f3.

McKissack, Patricia C., and Fredrick McKissack, Jr. *Black
Diamond: The Story of the Negro Baseball Leagues*. New
York: Scholastic, 1994.

Nathanson, Mitchell. *A People's History of Baseball*.
Champaign, IL: University of Illinois Press, 2012.

National Archives. "Jackie Robinson: Civil Rights Advocate. Letter: Jackie Robinson to Lyndon B. Johnson, April 18, 1967." Accessed September 3, 2018. https://www.archives.gov/education/lessons/jackie-robinson/letter-1967.html

Rampersad, Arnold. *Jackie Robinson: A Biography*. New York: Ballantine, 1997.

Ricks, Thomas E. "Racial Inclusion and Diversity in the Armed Forces: Some Thoughts on Today." *Foreign Policy*, October 6, 2016. https://foreignpolicy.com/2016/10/06/racial-inclusion-and-diversity-in-the-armed-forces-some-thoughts-on-today.

Robinson, Jackie. *I Never Had It Made*: *An Autobiography*. New York: HarperCollins, 1995.

Robinson, Sharon. *Stealing Home: An Intimate Family Portrait by the Daughter of Jackie Robinson*. New York: HarperCollins, 1996.

Sauer, Patrick. "The Year of Jackie Robinson's Mutual Love Affair with Montreal." *Smithsonian*, April 6, 2015. https://www.smithsonianmag.com/history/year-jackie-robinsons-mutual-love-affair-montreal-180954878.

Simon, Scott. *Jackie Robinson and the Integration of Baseball*. Hoboken, NJ: John Wiley & Sons, 2002.

Sullivan, Paul. "President Obama's Words of Unity Inspire Cubs During White House Celebration." *Chicago Tribune*, January 18, 2017. http://www.chicagotribune.com/sports/

baseball/cubs/ct-obama-sports-cubs-white-house-spt-
0117-20170116-story.html.

Teitelbaum, Michael. *Jackie Robinson: Champion for Equality*.
New York: Sterling, 2010.

Tygiel, Jules. *Baseball's Great Experiment: Jackie Robinson and
His Legacy*. New York: Oxford University Press, 1997.

Tygiel, Jules, ed. *The Jackie Robinson Reader: Perspectives on an
American Hero*. New York: Dutton, 1997.

US Department of Defense. Defense Equal Opportunity
Management Institute. *Historical Overview of Racism in
the Military*. Florida, 2002. http://www.dtic.mil/dtic/tr/
fulltext/u2/a488652.pdf

Vernon, John. "Jim Crow, Meet Lieutenant Robinson."
Prologue, Spring, 2008. https://www.archives.gov/
publications/prologue/2008/spring/robinson.html.

Weaver, Bill L. "The Black Press and the Assault
on Professional Baseball's 'Color Line,' October,
1945-April, 1947." *Phylon* 40, no. 4 (1979): 303-17.
doi:10.2307/274527.

Will, George F. *Bunts*. New York: Touchstone, 1998.

INDEX

Grand Slam, 70
Greenberg, Hank, 54, 80
gridiron, 31, 70

Honolulu Bears, 34

integrate, 7, 39–42, 48, 50,
    55–56, 59, 62, 66, 68,
    70–71, 77, 89, 95

Jim Crow laws, 15–16, **17**, 24,
    29, 38, 44, 47–48
Johnson, Andrew, 12

Kansas City Monarchs, 39,
    40, 61
Ku Klux Klan, 20

letter, 31
Lincoln, President Abraham,
    11, 12, 27
Louis, Joe, 36
lynch, 17–18, 20, 68, 97

Major League Baseball
    (MLB), 5–7, 24, 33, 39,
    41–42, 48, 53, 55–56,
    61–62, 68, 71, 74, 82, 85,
    87, 95, 99
manager, 24, 39, 41, 66, 71,
    74, 78, 80
momentous, 41

Montreal Royals, 57, 62–63,
    71

National Association for the
    Advancement of Colored
    People (NAACP), 18, 21,
    44, 88
National Youth
    Administration (NYA),
    33–34

officer candidate school
    (OCS), 34, 36
Olympic Games, 30–31,
    97–98, **98**, **100**

Parks, Rosa, 44
PhD, 18
platform, 50
Plessy v. Ferguson, 16
progressive, 48, 50
Pulitzer Prize, 85

Reconstruction, 12, 14–15
Reese, Pee Wee, 71, 83, **84**
renaissance, 41
Rickey, Branch, 6, 39, 41, **46**,
    52, 56–59, **58**, 62–63, 71,
    77, 81–82, 87, 93–95
Robeson, Paul, 48, 89
Robinson, Mack, **29**, 30–31,
    33

ABOUT THE AUTHOR

When she was a small child, **Avery Elizabeth Hurt** would fall asleep listening to the sounds of baseball games on television and the radio. Her mother told her all the stories of baseball's great history, including ones that involved her own family. When she grew older, she stayed awake—even for extra innings. Now she writes about science and history for kids and young adults—and about baseball whenever she gets a chance. These days, she roots for her home team, the Birmingham Barons, in Birmingham, Alabama.